How to use *explore*

Issue 106

The 91 daily readings in this issue of Explore are designed to help you understand and apply the Bible as you read it each day.

It's serious!

We suggest that you allow 15 minutes each day to work through the Bible passage with the notes. It should be a meal, not a snack! Readings from other parts of the Bible can throw valuable light on the study passage. These cross-references can be skipped if you are already feeling full up, but will expand your grasp of the Bible. Explore uses the NIV2011 Bible translation, but you can also use it with the NIV1984 or ESV translations.

Sometimes a prayer box will encourage you to stop and pray through the lessons—but it is always important to allow time to pray for God's Spirit to bring his word to life, and to shape the way we think and live through it.

We're serious!

All of us who work on Explore share a passion for getting the Bible into people's lives. We fiercely hold to the Bible as God's word—to honour and follow, not to explain away.

1 Find a ti... you can rea... Bible each ...

2 Find a place where you can be quiet and think

3 Ask God to help you understand

4 Carefully read through the Bible passage for today

5 Study the verses with *Explore*, taking time to think

6 Pray about what you have read

thegoodbook COMPANY

BIBLICAL | RELEVANT | ACCESSIBLE

Welcome to **explore**

Being a Christian isn't a skill you learn, nor is it a lifestyle choice. It's about having a real relationship with the living God through his Son, Jesus Christ. The Bible tells us that this relationship is like a marriage.

It's important to start with this, because it is easy to view the practice of daily Bible reading as a Christian duty, or a hard discipline that is just one more thing to get done in our busy lives.

But the Bible is God speaking to us: opening his mind to us on how he thinks, what he wants for us and what his plans are for the world. And most importantly, it tells us what he has done for us in sending his Son, Jesus Christ, into the world. It's the way that the Spirit shows Jesus to us, and changes us as we behold his glory.

Here are a few suggestions for making your time with God more of a joy than a burden:

- *Time:* Find a time when you will not be disturbed. Many people have found that the morning is the best time as it sets you up for the day. But whatever works for you is right for you.

- *Place:* Jesus says that we are not to make a great show of our religion *(see Matthew 6:5-6)*, but rather, to pray with the door to our room shut. Some people plan to get to work a few minutes earlier and get their Bible out in an office or some other quiet corner.

- *Prayer:* Although *Explore* helps with specific prayer ideas from the passage, do try to develop your own lists to pray through. Use the flap inside the back cover to help with this. And allow what you read in the Scriptures to shape what you pray for yourself, the world and others.

- *Feast:* You can use the "Bible in a year" line at the bottom of each page to help guide you through the entire Scriptures throughout 2024. This year, the passages each day are linked, showing how God makes and keeps his promises. We're grateful to Katherine Fedor of treasureinthebible.com for her permission to use this Bible-reading plan. You'll find passages to read six days a week—Sunday is a "day off", or a day to catch up!

- *Share:* As the saying goes, *expression deepens impression*. So try to cultivate the habit of sharing with others what you have learned. Why not join our Facebook group to share your encouragements, questions and prayer requests? Search for *Explore: For your daily walk with God.*

And enjoy it! As you read God's word and God's Spirit works in your mind and your heart, you are going to see Jesus, and appreciate more of his love for you and his promises to you. That's amazing!

Carl Laferton is the Editorial Director of The Good Book Company

PHILIPPIANS: Confident

Welcome to Philippians: an intensely personal, joy-producing, gospel-focused, doctrinally-rich, prayer-inclining, holiness-growing, eternity-gazing book!

Writer and recipients

Read Philippians 1:1-2

❷ *How does Paul describe himself and Timothy (v 1)?*

❷ *How does he describe his recipients (v 1)?*

The word Paul uses to describe himself is literally "slave". He sees himself as a slave, bought by a master to be his possession. Of course, to serve such a master—the Master who died out of love for his "slaves"—is neither restrictive nor an imposition. The great paradox is that such slavery brings true freedom—from fear, futility and death.

Partners

Read Philippians 1:3-6

❷ *Why is Paul joyfully thanking God for the Philippian Christians?*

This word "partnership" (*koinonia*) means to share something in common with another person. Such a partnership occurs when two or more people become involved in a joint venture. This was the case with Peter, Andrew, James and John—partners in the same fishing business (Luke 5:3-11). They were, literally, in the same boat together. This is much like what Paul shares in common with the Philippians. Though separated by many miles, they remain in partnership, being fishers of men and sharing the message of salvation with the world.

This participation in the gospel is what all believers share together. We are in the same boat, engaged in the same profession, and we have a great deal in common with our partners, no matter what the differences are in our languages, cultures and experiences.

❷ *What is Paul confident of (Philippians 1:6)?*

❷ *Why would he need to have this confidence in order to thank God for them with joy, rather than with anxiety?*

Salvation is not a matter of our working for God's acceptance, but it is God working for us and in us. From beginning to end, salvation is entirely a divine work of grace. If God has caused you to be born again, you can be assured that he will carry on this work until "the day of Christ Jesus". As a believer in Christ, you are as certain of heaven as though you have already been there 10,000 years. God finishes what he starts.

⌄ Apply

❷ *How does verse 6 comfort you...*
- *when you consider your sins?*
- *as you think about the parts of your life that you find hard?*
- *as you pray for Christians you know?*

⌃ Pray

About whom will you "pray with joy" today, because of their partnership in the gospel with you?

Bible in a year: Deuteronomy 22 – 24 • Mark 10

Love prays

In this passage, Paul continues to tell the Philippians how he feels about them, and what he is praying for them.

Giving thanks

Read Philippians 1:7-8

> ❓ *How does Paul feel about the members of this church, and why?*

Real, deep affection for others must mark our lives, too. We must do more than simply endure, tolerate or be nice to other believers. We must lovingly care for them. No matter how doctrinally sound we may be, if we are without love, all our Christian service is "nothing" (1 Corinthians 13:1).

▾ Apply

> ❓ *As you look at your own feelings and life, does this truth encourage or challenge you, or both? Why?*

Prayer requests

Read Philippians 1:9-11

Think about the stages of Paul's prayer as he lays it out here.

> ❓ *What do you understand by each part?*
>
> ❓ *What is the end product—the chief aim—of what he is asking God to do in the Philippians?*

The greatest thing we can ask God to do for other Christians is to deepen their love for him and for others. Where love for each other grows, the church is most like heaven and becomes more attractive to the world.

"Knowledge" does not refer to the mere head knowledge of facts. It means having a heart understanding of people's lives that perceives their deepest needs and how we can best meet those needs. Paul is not praying that the Philippians would become smarter in their understanding, but wiser in their care for one another.

"Pure" is better translated "sincere", which comes from two words for "sun" and "to judge". It described a piece of fine pottery that was judged in the light of the sun and found to be without cracks. In ancient times, devious merchants would conceal flaws in their expensive pottery with wax. The authenticity of valuable pottery was revealed when held up to the light of the sun.

So Paul is praying for lives of integrity—that his friends will have a love that is real, and which, when it comes into contact with the heat of a difficult situation or a person who demands sacrifice or commitment, does not melt away. It speaks of a character that does not crack under pressure.

And all this will lead to God being praised (v 11). He alone is worthy of all praise—and so the pursuit and promotion of his glory must be our all-consuming passion.

▴ Pray

Make Paul's prayer your prayer, both for yourself and also for members of your church.

Joy in jail

Paul is in difficult circumstances—he has been arrested and sent to Rome, has suffered shipwreck, and has been imprisoned. Yet he is rejoicing. How can this be?

Possibilities not problems

Read Philippians 1:12-14

❷ *What does Paul want the Philippians to know (v 12)?*

❷ *What two results have his "chains" had (v 13-14)?*

No matter in what hard place we may find ourselves, God can use us to advance his word in that very situation. Where is it that you feel restricted in life? Wherever you find yourself, you can see your adverse situation as an opportunity to give testimony for Christ where one might not otherwise exist. You are not where you are by accident. You are where you are by divine appointment, for the purposes of sharing the gospel.

A higher agenda

Read Philippians 1:15-18a

❷ *Why does Paul not mind some Christians who envy him making trouble for him by preaching the gospel (v 18)?*

This is the third time in these verses that Paul speaks of Christ being proclaimed. The priority for Paul is always the magnification of his Master. He is not preoccupied with escaping his suffering, nor with rebutting his foes. Paul has a much higher agenda.

❷ *Why is it liberating to live caring more about our Redeemer than our own reputation?*

Confidence

Read Philippians 1:18b-20

❷ *What does Paul:*
　• *know (v 19)?*
　• *expect (v 20)?*

❷ *How can this give him confidence as he faces his trial before Caesar?*

He will soon be released from this imprisonment and trial one way or another, either by death or by dismissal. Paul believes that his life is held in the hands of the sovereign God. It is this conviction in the overruling authority of God that gives him great joy. He would be filled with fear if he did not trust in this powerful truth. He would have no joy if he thought that his circumstances were governed by mere random chance. Paul lays his head on the pillow of the sovereignty of God each night—and he sleeps well on it.

⌄ Apply

❷ *How has Paul's perspective on life in these verses...*
　• *comforted you?*
　• *changed your own perspective?*
　• *motivated you to share the gospel today?*

❷ *What will it look like for you to lay your head on the "pillow" of the sovereignty of God tonight?*

To live is…

No one is ready to live until they are ready to die. The end of your life must be secure before the present can be stable.

Read Philippians 1:21-26

The focus

❓ *What is Paul's preoccupying focus in life (v 21)?*

❓ *What is Paul's attitude towards death (v 21)?*

❓ *Why does he view the end of his earthly life in this way (v 23)?*

Paul's life is, in a sense, flashing before his eyes. In such a sobering situation, Paul sums up what that life is really all about. Everything in his life is bound up in Christ. The passionate pursuit of his whole being is to know and glorify Christ. The sum and substance of his present state is confined in Christ. Every moment of every day is lived for Christ.

This is what it means to be a Christian. It involves living primarily and pre-eminently for Christ. Everything else in life is secondary.

Paul is only able to live this way because of his view of his death. For him, to die is a far greater gain than living. Why? Because the grave will graduate him to glory. It will not be a tragedy but a triumph—and that is the secret to living confidently as a Christian. As the Puritan Richard Sibbes wrote:

What greater encouragement can a man have to fight against his enemy than when he is sure of the victory before he fights?

Notice that what is most important in heaven is not the streets of gold, nor the gates of pearl. The greatest gain of being in heaven is not even to be reunited with loved ones. The greatest profit will be to stand before Christ and behold him as he is (v 23). The glory of heaven is found in Jesus Christ himself. Death will bring Paul to the Lord Jesus Christ. What greater gain can there be than this?

The dilemma

❓ *What is Paul's dilemma (v 22-23)?*

❓ *What does he decide, and why (v 24-26)?*

⌄ Apply

❓ *What would change in your life if you saw it as Paul saw his—all about Christ, with death as a greater gain?*

❓ *Which verse from this section would be most helpful for you to commit to memory, and when do you think you will most need to recall it and live it out?*

❓ *Are you ready to die?*

⌃ Pray

Lord, thank you that, by faith in your Son, when I die I shall see him face to face. Please would my heart cry be, "To live is Christ; to die is gain". Please would my purpose for being alive today be to live completely for him. Amen.

 Bible in a year: Deuteronomy 29 – 30 • Jeremiah 4 • Psalm 25

Good, not easy, news

Here is a reminder of the price every believer must pay if they are to walk in a manner worthy of their calling. The gospel is good news; but it is never easy news.

Read Philippians 1:27-30

❓ *What will the Christian life look like, according to Paul's words here?*

Consistent Christianity

"Conduct yourselves" (v 27) means to live as the citizen of a country in a law-abiding manner. We must live consistently with what we believe; otherwise we will be a walking contradiction in terms. "Whatever happens" in your life, this command is for you.

Standing together

❓ *What report about the Philippian church does Paul want to hear (v 27)?*

❓ *What will this be a sign of—for them, and for their opponents (v 28)?*

The opponents of the Philippian Christians are the false teachers who have infiltrated the church with their corrupt teaching (3:1-2). If the believers in this church were not truly converted, they would give in instead of standing firm. The opposition demonstrates to the world the differences between what the true Christians and the Judaizers teach. (Judaizers thought the Old Testament Levitical law should still apply to all Christians.)

Suffering and salvation

❓ *What two things have been "granted", or given, to these Christians by God (1:29)?*

❓ *How should this shape our view of going through hardships in order to obey or proclaim the gospel?*

All who receive the former gift in verse 29 also receive the latter. These two are a package deal. All the believers in Philippi had been granted saving faith, as well as the privilege of suffering for the gospel. Paul wrote elsewhere, "Everyone who wants to live a godly life in Christ Jesus will be persecuted" (2 Timothy 3:12). Peter said we should rejoice in our sufferings and are blessed when we suffer for Jesus' sake (1 Peter 4:13-14). Suffering because of our salvation is to be expected and accepted.

⌄ Apply

Notice that all these things—standing, striving and suffering—are to be done "together" (Philippians 1:27).

❓ *How can you contribute to your church living in this way?*

❓ *How will you view suffering for Christ today?*

⌃ Pray

Thank God for the gift of faith through believing the gospel. Thank him for the gift of suffering for the cause of the gospel. Pray that whatever happens today, you would conduct yourself in a manner that is pleasing to Christ.

Bible in a year: Deuteronomy 31 – 33 • Ephesians 1

He exalts the humble

Perhaps the greatest apparent contradiction of the Christian life is before us in this chapter of Philippians: we must humble ourselves if we are to be exalted.

"Humility" is a word that means we think of or judge ourselves with lowliness. The idea is this: "do not think of yourself more highly than you ought, but rather think of yourself with sober judgment" (Romans 12:3). True humility is a central tenet of the Christian faith. No one struts through the narrow gate that leads into the kingdom. We are sheep, not peacocks; servants, not sovereigns.

The call to humility

Read Philippians 2:1-4

❓ *What does it mean to live with Christian humility?* • v 2   • v 3   • v 4

The word "if" in verse 1 can also be translated as "since" or "because".

❓ *What is the link between the truth of what we enjoy (v 1) and the lifestyle Paul commands in verses 2-4?*

The supreme example

Where do we look to see humility worked out in life? Supremely, in the life of the Lord Jesus...

Read Philippians 2:5-8

Paul writes that Christ "humbled himself" (v 8).

❓ *Where did Christ begin, and what downward steps did he take (v 6-8)?*

❓ *What are we to do (v 5)?*

If the Son of God lowered himself humbly in order to serve others, how can you and I not be willing? We must make whatever sacrifice is necessary for the good of others. None of us will ever surpass the humility of Christ. None of us may ever say, "Enough. I deserve better, so I will stop here."

What God does

Read Philippians 2:9-11

❓ *After the humiliation of Christ, what happened next (v 9-11)?*

The point is that no one ever truly humbles themselves before God without being exalted by God, whether in this life or in the life to come. True humility will never be forgotten by God. God will see it, God will note it, and God will reward it. It is one thing to be exalted by man, but it is something else entirely, and eternally, to be exalted by God. This is the essence of true humility—to accept that it is our status before God which is of ultimate importance.

⌄ Apply

❓ *How have these verses challenged you about your own attitude to yourself, and to others?*

❓ *How have they motivated you to live humbly?*

❓ *What do you need to pray about right now?*

 Bible in a year: Deuteronomy 34 • Joshua 1 • Hebrews 3 • Revelation 15

What is man?

John Calvin said that we cannot know ourselves if we do not know God, and cannot know God if we do not know ourselves. This psalm enables us to know both.

Read Psalm 8

❷ *What impression of God does David want us to have (v 1, 9)?*

Who is he?

❷ *Where can God's glory be heard, or seen?*

• *v 1b*   • *v 2*   • *v 3*

When we consider the greatness of God and the vastness of his creation, we must start to feel our own smallness. The question of verse 4 comes to all our lips from time to time: why would God be bothered about us? Who are we, tiny specks in the grand cosmos, that the Creator should care for us?

Who are we?

❷ *What position did God give us (v 5)?*

❷ *What purpose did God give us (v 6-8)?*

Humans were not an afterthought or a random addition in the great creating works of God. **Read Genesis 1:26-29.** We are not mere specks; we are cared-for creatures, given the privileged position of knowing God, and the privileged purpose of caring for his creation. The tragedy is that, because we do not like to be dependent upon or subject to anyone, we reject our created-ness—relegating ourselves to mere matter, which does not matter much. It is only if we realise how small we are in God's creation that we realise how valued we are in God's sight.

Who shall we be?

Read Hebrews 2:5-10

The writer of Hebrews, writing to 1st-century Christians, quotes Psalm 8 to them.

❷ *What does he say God did (middle v 8)?*

❷ *But what do we not see (end v 8)?*

In trying to rule the world without God, we as humanity forfeited our ability to rule the world under God. There is a great mismatch between what Psalm 8 says about the earth, and what we see on the earth—humans are not perfectly ruling God's creation…

❷ *But what do we "see" (Hebrews 2:9)?*

There is a perfect human, who came from heaven and was made lower than the angels, who died for his people to restore them to relationship with God, and who was crowned with glory and honour. Jesus will rule "the world to come"—and will restore us, God's "sons and daughters", to the people we were created to be, ruling alongside him in his recreated world.

Apply

❷ *How does Psalm 8:4-8 teach us to see ourselves with humble dignity?*

❷ *How do verses 6-8 help you to go to work with purpose today or tomorrow?*

❷ *How does Hebrews 2 prompt you to look forward to the world to come with excitement?*

From now till heaven

What takes place in my life after being saved and before going to heaven? In two verses, Paul has much to teach us about the nature of the Christian life.

Read Philippians 2:12-13

Paul begins this section, "Therefore, my dear friends" (v 12). This is addressed exclusively to Christians. If we miss this point, it will lead us to falsely see these verses as teaching that someone must work to earn their salvation. Paul is speaking to those already saved by faith in Christ.

Working it out

❓ *What does he tell Christians to do (v 12)?*

They were not to work for their salvation, but to work out their salvation. They were to work out what God had already worked in. Being a believer who is saved by God's grace does not negate your responsibility to keep God's moral law, outlined in his word. A firm, uncompromising commitment to obeying the word, accompanied by true, serious repentance when you fail, are two marks of a true believer who has been born again (1 John 2:3-6).

Joyful awe

❓ *What attitude should Christians have as they work out their salvation (end Philippians 2:12)?*

❓ *Why (v 13)?*

The end of verse 12 describes a wholesome, healthy, reverential awe for God and a sober realisation of the need to take him seriously.

Note that this "fear and trembling" is recorded in a letter that continually emphasises joy in Christian living. The gladness that believers experience in the Lord grows out of the fertile soil of fearing God with reverential awe. God is not a kindly spiritual grandfather, sitting in the sky. God is not a kitten. God is a lion who loves us, but his love does not mean we are at liberty to domesticate him. Because of this, we are called to tremble joyfully in our walk with God.

The workers

❓ *Who is at work to grow the Philippians in holiness (v 12-13)?*

The idea is that God's will takes the initiative and is acting upon their will. The divine work in them is what is causing them to work in sanctification. The soul of each believer is the field of labour of this sanctifying work. It is God who is working in them, bringing a gracious force to bear upon their wills.

☑ Apply

❓ *In which areas do you need to work particularly hard on applying your salvation to your life?*

❓ *How will this cause you to pray for God to be at work in you?*

Shine

Building upon his foundational teaching on growing in holiness and obedience (v 12-13), Paul now gives us some specific application for daily living.

Everything without...

Read Philippians 2:14

❷ *Why is "everything" a challenging word?*

"Grumbling" means murmuring or muttering. It refers to private complaining under your breath. "Arguing" speaks of a contentious spirit that feels the need to be continually questioning what is done in the church.

☑ Apply

❷ *About what do you find it easiest to grumble and/or argue?*

❷ *Are you going to stop?*

So you may become...

Read Philippians 2:15

❷ *Why is it important not to grumble or argue?*

"Blameless" here means that no accusation can be brought against us when it comes to grumbling or arguing.

❷ *How will living this way, as "children of God", mean we are different to the world around us?*

☑ Apply

❷ *In what ways do you find it most tempting to blend in with the darkness of your generation? What would change*

if you saw those areas of temptation as opportunities to stand out and shine more brightly?

The word of life

Read Philippians 2:16-18

"Hold firmly to" more correctly carries the idea of "hold forth". The idea is not merely that we would have a tenacious grip on the gospel, but would also extend the gospel to others.

A drink offering (v 17) was a sacrifice that was poured on top of an animal sacrifice (Exodus 29:38-41). The steam from the liquid symbolised the rising of the sacrificial offering to God. So Paul's life is being poured out in order that the Philippians' lives might be offered in sacrifice to God.

❷ *How will Paul feel as he hears of the Philippian Christians shining like stars and holding to / holding forth the "word of life" (Philippians 2:16-18)?*

☑ Apply

Our distinctive lives provide the platform for us to testify with our mouths.

❷ *With whom will you actively seek to share the gospel this week?*

❷ *How have verses 14-18 encouraged and challenged you about how you are working out your salvation in your life?*

Real-life humility

Paul gave us the supreme example of humility of mind in the Lord Jesus (v 5-11). Now we come to two more real-life examples: Timothy and Epaphroditus.

Timothy

Read Philippians 2:19-24

Paul is in prison in Rome, and Timothy is right there with him. The apostle is not a popular person to be associated with right now. Timothy, nevertheless, is with him. Where others have left, Timothy has lasted.

> ❓ *What does humility look like (v 20-21)?*

Paul points out that the Philippians "know" about Timothy's humility, because he has "proved himself" (v 22). For years, Timothy has been battle-tested with Paul on the front lines of spiritual warfare. Though he is relatively young—only in his mid-thirties—he has been well educated in the school of hard ministry knocks and has passed with flying colours. Timothy has the spiritual scars to prove his advanced degree.

⌄ Apply

Every trial that you undergo is intended to prepare you for future service. God always has refining purposes in the midst of your difficulties. Your hardships are the training school for your ministry.

> ❓ *How does this affect the way you look at the difficulties or disappointments in your life?*
>
> ❓ *Can you see how the Lord might be growing you in humility in order to prepare you to serve?*

⌃ Pray

If we are to be profitable servants, we must be self-denying, and not self-focused. We must be large-hearted, just as Timothy was. Ask God to enlarge your heart for others. Ask for grace to care more for their welfare than for your comfort or reputation.

Epaphroditus

Read Philippians 2:25-30

> ❓ *What had happened to Epaphroditus while he was with Paul (v 27)?*
>
> ❓ *What is amazing about how Epaphroditus felt about his life-threatening illness (v 26)?*
>
> ❓ *How should we respond to people like this (v 29)?*

⌄ Apply

Through his word, God asks us to look at these two men and consider what it looks like to place the interests of others above our own—to live with Christ-like humility. These servants of Christ are held up before us as those whom we should emulate.

> ❓ *What would it look like for your life to be given to God in humility in a manner worthy of the commendations given by Paul of Timothy and Epaphroditus?*
>
> ❓ *If you had to explain what humility is and how humble people live, how would you use Philippians 2 to do so?*

Bible in a year: Joshua 9 – 11 • 2 Corinthians 10

True joy

A Christian possesses joy that the world never knows.

Joy is completely different from happiness. Happiness is entirely based upon the circumstances of life. Happiness is fleeting, temporary and fragile. Authentic Christian joy comes from having a personal relationship with God through Jesus Christ. This source of joy rises above our circumstances and cannot be drained by the surrounding situation. Happiness flees in the hard times. Joy endures.

❷ *Have there been times where you had little happiness and yet great joy?*

The joy command

Read Philippians 3:1

❷ *Who is Paul addressing, and what does he tell them to do?*

This joy is *restricted* to those who have been supernaturally born again into God's family. But this joy is *available* to all those who have been born again—whether they are male or female, young or old.

Notice that this is a command to be obeyed. Paul's readers may not have felt like rejoicing, but that did not give them an excuse to mope around. There are reasons why we become discouraged, some of them significant. But there are always greater reasons to rejoice. God does not command what he does not make possible.

❷ *Where do we find joy, according to the first sentence of verse 1?*

Watch out!

Read Philippians 3:2-3

❷ *Who does Paul warn the Philippians to "watch out for" (v 2)? What do you make of the words he chooses to use?*

These false teachers are seeking to impose circumcision on the Christians as a requirement for salvation. They are teaching that human works must be added to faith alone in Christ alone in order to receive salvation.

Imagine that you believed that you need to do something as well as trust Christ in order to be saved from hell, for heaven.

❷ *How would that steal the joy from life?*

But, Paul says, in knowing Christ we are "the circumcision"—we have had our old, sinful hearts cut out, which is what the rite of circumcision always pointed to. We are those who can truly worship God. We are those who "boast in Christ Jesus"—who find our confidence in who he is and all he has done.

❷ *How does approaching life in this way only ever increase your joy?*

⌃ Pray

Whether you feel happy or unhappy right now, pray that God would show you all you enjoy in Christ, so that knowing him would be your greatest and your unfading joy.

BC to AD

Every believer has a testimony of how they came to faith in Jesus Christ. In these verses, Paul presents his to us.

He gives us "Vol. One: BC (Before Christ)" and "Vol. Two: AD (After Deliverance)".

Before Christ

Read Philippians 3:4-6

What Paul means by verse 4 is, *If anyone could be accepted by God on the basis of their own efforts, I am at the head of that list.*

- ❓ *What was impressive about his background and behaviour (v 5-6)?*
- ❓ *What would the equivalent person in your time and place be like?*

Paul had everything—except Jesus Christ. But, as he was about to discover, if a person does not have Christ, they have nothing. He had everything except everything he needed.

⌄ Apply

- ❓ *How would you describe your life before you were converted to faith in Christ?*
- ❓ *Are you reading this and realising that you are, right now, a religious person who does not actually have a personal trust in Christ as your Saviour and Lord?*

After Deliverance

Read Philippians 3:7-9

- ❓ *How does Paul now view what he once put such confidence in, and why (v 7)?*

- ❓ *How does he compare these things to knowing Jesus, and why (v 8-9)?*

Paul is describing the change caused by his conversion. **Read Acts 9:1-19.** There may be a process that leads up to conversion, but there is a moment when we cross the line; we step out of the world and step into the kingdom of heaven. Every Christian has a story of conversion.

Paul was not seeking after God—but, in Jesus Christ, God was seeking him. Our part in our conversion was to run away from Jesus, whether we did so politely, religiously or aggressively. Christ's part was to run after us, bring us low and show us who he is and what he offers.

This must be our testimony. We may never say, "I was looking for God, and I found him". We may only ever testify, "I was not looking for any God other than myself—and he found me". You did not work it out. He sought you out and he saved your soul.

⌄ Apply

- ❓ *How would you describe the way in which Jesus did this for you?*
- ❓ *With whom could you share your testimony?*

⌃ Pray

- ❓ *As you reflect on your "BC" and your "AD", how does it move you to thank God?*

Marks of new life

Having recounted his conversion, Paul continues by describing his life post-conversion. In the next two studies we will see four distinguishing marks of new life in Christ.

A new priority

Read Philippians 3:10

❷ *What does Paul now most want?*

If he already knows Christ, why does he want to know him whom he already knows? The answer is that he wants to know Christ more deeply, and have a more intimate relationship with him. He wants to learn more of his teaching and draw closer to his heart. He wants to enter into a closer, experiential fellowship—a more intimate communion. "For to me, to live is Christ" (1:21). The whole life, the highest aim and the greatest priority of the apostle, and for us today as believers, is knowing Christ.

⌃ Pray

❷ *Is there any danger that you know about Christ intellectually, rather than knowing him personally?*

Pray now that, by his Spirit, you would know Christ more and more intimately, and joyfully.

A new power

❷ *What power does Paul now look to (3:10)?*

He does not want to live a mundane Christian life that could be easily explained by his own natural abilities. Instead, he wants to be a powerhouse for Christ, to exert a spiritual influence upon the world and to see transformation in others. Only life-giving, death-defying power will do this.

❷ *What kind of life is Paul expecting?*

As Martin Luther is reputed to have said, "They gave our Master a crown of thorns. Why do we hope for a crown of roses?"

⌄ Apply

❷ *Why is this perspective on our lives both challenging and liberating?*

❷ *How does it help you to suffer for the gospel today?*

A new prospect

Read Philippians 3:11

❷ *What is Paul looking forward to?*

"Somehow" does not mean that Paul is not sure he will attain this wonderful future; it is that he does not know the path God will lead him on between today and that glorious day. But though the route is unclear, the destination is certain.

⌃ Pray

Look forward to the day that you attain "to the resurrection from the dead" and praise God for your future, even as you ask him for help to be faithful in the struggles of your present.

Bible in a year: Joshua 18 – 20 • Psalm 37

Praise while persecuted

This is a psalm that teaches us to place our present struggles in the wider context of who God is, and what God has done and will do.

Read Psalm 9:1-2, 13

> ❓ *What is going on right now in David's life (v 13a)?*
>
> ❓ *So why is it remarkable that he begins with verses 1-2?*

How wonderful to be able to know gladness and joy, and wholehearted praise, even when facing persecution. But how do we manage to actually do this?

Read Psalm 9:3-20

Verses 3-6 seem to be looking back to past times.

> ❓ *What has God done for David previously (v 3-6)?*

Verses 7-10 switch the focus back to the present, but also upwards towards God.

> ❓ *What is God doing right now, even as David faces persecution (v 7-9)?*
>
> ❓ *What can his people be confident about, even as they face persecution (v 10)?*

We often find ourselves explaining away or apologising for the truth that God is a God of judgment—but David celebrates it, and so should we. It is great news that God remembers what people have done to each other, and that he does not ignore those who cry out in affliction (v 12). Those who commit evil and escape justice in this world will not escape it in the next, because God does not forget and he does not ignore it.

> ❓ *What does David ask God to do (v 13)?*

> ❓ *What does David want to do (v 14)?*

"Daughter Zion" is a term for Jerusalem, the city of God's presence among his people. David is asking his Lord to turn him back from the gates of death, so that he can be brought through the gates into Jerusalem. Living this side of Jesus' ministry, we can confidently ask for even more—that God would bring us through the gates of death and out beyond them through the gates into his eternal presence. The wicked will go "down to the realm of the dead" (v 17), but God will bring us to his presence, where we will enjoy salvation and sing his praises. The nations—the enemies of David and his God—are "only mortal" (v 20). The Lord, on the other hand, "reigns for ever" (v 7).

⌄ Apply

Think of a struggle you are currently experiencing—it might be persecution, or pain, or disappointment, or betrayal.

> ❓ *Can you think of times of struggle God has brought you through in the past? Can you praise him for that now?*
>
> ❓ *Can you remember that, whatever happens, as you cling to him he will bring you through death and into the heavenly Jerusalem? How will that change your view of your present suffering?*
>
> ❓ *Can you begin to pray (even if you don't much feel like it) the words of verses 1-2?*

Running hard

Paul has a new priority, a new power, a new prospect—and a new pursuit. That's the focus of the next few verses.

A new pursuit

Read Philippians 3:12-14

- ❷ *What is Paul pressing on towards (v 12, 14)?*
- ❷ *What "one thing" does this involve doing (v 13)?*
- ❷ *What do you think this means in real life when he...*
  - *sins?*
  - *faces disappointment?*
  - *enjoys success?*

"Press on" is a phrase used of a sprinter running a race. Like a runner pressing on to the finish line, Paul is all-out in his effort to pursue Christ. He understood that Christ Jesus had laid hold of him on the Damascus road, and that he must press forward and lay hold of Christ every day of his life.

As with any race, the prize is received at the end of the race, not during it. When he crosses the finish line—the line between this life and heaven—that is when he will be given the prize. When Paul receives this upward call, he will not be found shuffling down the track. He will be sprinting at full speed to the finish line.

If you think differently

Read Philippians 3:15-17

- ❷ *What will Christian maturity look like (v 15)?*
- ❷ *What helps us grow in maturity (v 17)?*

At the end of verse 15, Paul is alluding to the fact that there has been wrong thinking about the need to press on. He is confident that God will make this known to them. For whatever reason, some of the Philippians have stopped running the race of faith with wholehearted effort. They have succumbed to a sluggish mentality in their Christian lives and have become slack in their pursuit of holiness. So Paul says that God will reveal this different attitude to them—he will highlight their passivity. They need to be shown their need to push themselves harder in their quest for maturity—and they need to follow a pace-setter (v 17).

⌄ Apply

- ❷ *Ask yourself:*
  - *Is God right now revealing in you an apathetic attitude towards your Christian life?*
  - *Have you become undisciplined in your Bible-reading and study? Or careless in your prayer life?*
  - *Have you become half-hearted in witnessing for Jesus Christ?*
  - *Does there need to be an adjustment in your attitude?*

Increasing Christ-likeness—until the day we cross the finish line into Christ's presence, is too great a prize to let slip. If you are slowing, strolling or even sitting down in the middle of the track, stand up and start running.

Bible in a year: Joshua 21 – 23 • Psalm 33

Citizens of another city

Just as we must find good examples to emulate (v 17), we must also realise that there are bad examples to avoid, because there is a wonderful future to be prized.

Enemies of the cross

Read Philippians 3:18-19

❓ *How is Paul feeling as he writes?*

❓ *How does his description of these people underline the seriousness of their way of life, and outline what drives them?*

To whom is Paul referring? Almost certainly the "Judaizers" at whom he took aim earlier in this chapter, who were bringing a negative influence and who were to be avoided like the plague. He writes "with tears" because he is broken-hearted at the harm they are inflicting on the church.

"Their god is their stomach" refers not to their physical hunger, but, metaphorically, to their sensual lusts. They worship what feels right, or what feels good. Their own desires are elevated to the level of divine authority in their lives.

▾ Apply

❓ *How do you see "stomach-god" teaching in your own culture or even in church?*

❓ *How about in your own heart?*

Citizens of heaven

Read Philippians 3:20-21

The "destiny" of living in the way described in verses 18-19 is "destruction".

❓ *What alternative destiny does Paul describe in verses 20-21?*

❓ *What particularly excites you about his words here?*

In the first century, Roman "citizenship" was sometimes given to people living in a foreign city or province far from Rome. Philippi was one such Roman colony, and its inhabitants were Roman citizens. But Paul is reminding them that their real citizenship is in another place. Their names are permanently recorded where the King of kings, Jesus Christ, is enthroned at the right hand of God. They are citizens of two distant cities—and Rome is not the greater.

❓ *How should citizens of heaven feel as they wait for Jesus to return (v 20)?*

This world is not our home. As we live here on earth, we must maintain our greater allegiance to our Lord Jesus, never caving in to the pressure to squeeze into the mould of this rebellious world. Instead, we must set our minds on things above, not upon things below. We are headed for home.

▾ Apply

❓ *How does considering your life in Jesus' kingdom when he returns encourage you to live as a citizen of his kingdom today?*

❓ *How does it undermine any temptation to live with your stomach, instead of your Saviour, as your Lord?*

Conflict management

Since the dawn of human history, beginning with Cain and Abel (Genesis 4:1-16),
there has been conflict between individuals. No church escapes this friction.

Wherever there are people, there is the potential for conflict. The church in Philippi was no different.

Read Philippians 4:1-5

The issue

In verse 2, Paul addresses the problem that was festering within this congregation. Putting his finger on the live nerve, he urges Euodia and Syntyche to "be of the same mind". Obviously, these two women were at odds with one another; and this squabble was serious enough that Paul incorporated it into this small letter of only four chapters.

❓ *What do we find out about Euodia and Syntyche in verse 3?*

These were not obscure members in the life of this flock. These were frontline warriors—servants who had put their shoulders to the plough in the cause of the gospel. They were true believers, whose names were, along with the rest of Paul's "co-workers", written "in the book of life" (v 3).

❓ *What effect could this conflict between two keen church members have had on the wider church, do you think?*

The way forward

❓ *What does Paul command others in the church to do in light of this conflict?*

•*v 1*   •*v 3*   •*v 4*   •*v 5*

❓ *How would obeying these commands help the church not to be overcome by this conflict?*

Paul realises it will be difficult for these two women to work this out. The wounds appear deep and the hurt has presumably been there for some time (otherwise Paul would not have heard about it). Consequently, he appeals to another member of the church in Philippi to step in and act as a peacemaker. A reconciler is needed, who will bring these two women together.

Not only this, but in this circumstance—as in all others—the Philippians must still "rejoice" (v 4). These in-house differences and disagreements should not prevent the Philippians from rejoicing. Most likely, rejoicing together may serve to heal the divide. Rejoicing in all the Lord is to us and for us tends to help us have the correct perspective on everything else, especially in conflict.

⌄ Apply

❓ *Do you need to take any decisive steps to make peace with a fellow believer? How will you do that today?*

❓ *Do you need to take any decisive steps to help some other believers make peace with each other? How will you do that today?*

An antidote for anxiety

Paul is chained to a soldier, in captivity 24 hours a day, seven days a week, and he has been in this situation for two years. He has every reason to worry—yet he is at peace.

Read Philippians 4:6-7

The anxiety command

❓ *Why do we find it so hard to obey the command at the start of verse 6?*

To be "anxious" means to be troubled with cares—to be pulled in different directions, or to be pulled apart. The picture is to suffer the tension of your hopes pulling in one direction and the trials of life pulling in the opposite direction.

This kind of anxiety works against us enjoying the truth that there is a sovereign God who keeps his promises and is at work in all things for our good.

The cure for anxiety

❓ *What primary cure for worry does Paul give in verse 6?*

Notice the all-encompassing nature of "anything" and "every situation". We can do something with our anxiety, no matter what is causing it—we can pray about "every situation" that troubles our peace and we can trust in God.

Read Matthew 6:25-34

❓ *How are Jesus' words here similar to Paul's in Philippians 4?*

❓ *What additional encouragements does the Lord give us here, in order to enable us to obey the command not to worry?*

Both Paul and Jesus are saying, *Trust God who will provide for your needs.* Prayer is a sign that we are willing to do this. It is worth asking yourself: what is there in my life that causes me some sense of panic? Realise that God is not worried. There is no panic in heaven, but only plans to work out his good purposes in your life. Remembering this and believing this is what can help us face our anxieties and fears.

The outcome

❓ *When we pray instead of panicking, what do we enjoy (Philippians 4:7)?*

When a Christian prays dependently, God may not change their circumstances, but he does change their heart. This is a precious promise for every Christian who knows what it is to be gripped by anxiety.

⌄ Apply

❓ *What are the main sources of your anxiety today, and how does it manifest itself in your emotions and your life? How attractive do you find the idea of knowing peace about those things?*

❓ *Why is it easy to decide that the Bible's challenge to our anxieties does not apply to our particular worries?*

❓ *How can you apply to your anxieties the cure for worry that Paul lays out here?*

Mind your mind

Now Paul reaches the climax of his appeal. "Finally, brothers and sisters…" he writes—
this is for all the believers in Philippi, and to every believer in every place.

Think about…

Read Philippians 4:8

❷ *What are we to "think about"—or, more literally, "dwell on" or "focus on"?*

❷ *What would the opposite of each of these things be?*

Ultimately, each of these virtues is a description of the Lord Jesus Christ. This is how he thought, constantly and consistently, in every circumstance and at every point. And so whatever meets this mark is acceptable and pleasing to God, but whatever falls short of this standard is unacceptable.

Thoughts matter. If we focus upon what is right, we will live rightly. If we focus upon what is wrong, we will live wrongly. There is an inseparable connection between what we think about and how we live. We cannot focus our minds on what is wrong and then live out what is right. The deposits that are being made into our minds are yielding a return with interest in our lives.

So we must guard our minds because we will soon become like that upon which we are thinking.

⌄ Apply

Reflect on the eight areas Paul tells you to think about.

❷ *To what extent are you already thinking this way?*

❷ *Are there ways you struggle to think like this? What are you dwelling on instead?*

❷ *How will you pursue godly thinking more proactively?*

Choose to imitate

Read Philippians 4:9

How do we put these defining marks into practice? One way is by seeing them lived out in the life of a more mature believer and imitating that. There is a direct connection between what is required in verse 8 and what Paul urges in verse 9. As the Philippians strive to dwell on what is acceptable, they should look to Paul and emulate him.

⌄ Apply

❷ *Who are you imitating? Have you made a conscious choice to seek to emulate a few people who are more godly, wise and mature than you?*

❷ *Are you imitable? Is your life one a younger Christian could look at and seek to follow? How, and how not?*

⌃ Pray

Thank Jesus that he is the perfect description of each of the qualities listed in verse 8. Pray about any that challenge you as you look at your own life. Thank him that, by his Spirit, he is able to change you to become more like him.

The key to contentment

Paul is a man who is content despite his circumstances, rather than being crushed by them. What is the secret of such contentment?

What Paul learned

Read Philippians 4:10-12

❓ *What was Paul doing (v 10)?*

❓ *Where was Paul (1:13-14)? How does this make 4:10-12 surprising?*

Genuine joy is found in the unchangeable Lord. Though life's affairs are always changing, the eternal purposes of God never change. Paul realises that he is in chains by divine appointment, and because of that he has every reason to rejoice.

❓ *What has Paul "learned" (v 11)?*

❓ *What "secret" has he discovered (v 12)?*

The word translated "content" here was used of a country where nothing had to be imported. Such a country had all the resources and natural products needed to be self-sufficient. Nothing else was needed from the outside. Paul is saying, *If I have God, I have all I need, and I am content.*

The secret

Read Philippians 4:13

❓ *What had Paul discovered?*

Jesus said, "Apart from me you can do nothing" (John 15:5). Paul has discovered that in him he can do everything.

Philippians 4:13 has been misunderstood—and misapplied—repeatedly over time. So it needs some qualification:

1. This does not mean God will empower me to sin.

2. This does not mean I can do supernatural physical feats, such as jump across the Atlantic or flap my arms and fly to the moon. "All this" means the things that we are called to do in order to obey God.

3. This does not relieve me of my responsibility to commit myself to the means of grace—God's word, God's meal at the Lord's Supper, and so on. If I just sit back passively, I am not going to know this strength. It requires my active pursuit of the means of grace for me to experience this supernatural power in my life.

But here is what this does mean: you can live your Christian life knowing that the power of God is far greater than whatever the difficulty is that you are facing. There is no trial too difficult. There is no obstacle too high. There is no temptation too strong. There is no opposition too powerful. There is no persecution too threatening. Put your faith and trust in God and follow him in obedience; this joy will be your joy, and this contentment will be your contentment, and this confidence will be your confidence.

⌄ Apply

You have all you can ever need in Christ, and you can do all things through Christ.

❓ *How does this truth speak to your soul today?*

Realistic but not hopeless

Sooner or later, all of us find ourselves asking the question this psalm begins with: "Why, LORD, do you stand far off?" In other words: Why, God, don't you help me?

Why stand far off?

Read Psalm 10:1-11

❓ *What is "the wicked man" doing to others (v 2, 8-10)?*

❓ *What is he saying about himself and about God (v 6, 11, see also v 13)?*

The writer is painting in vivid language a picture of someone who takes advantage of people weaker than them, uses their power for their own ends, and treads on others to elevate themselves, while refusing to believe that there is a God who sees, or cares, or will act. So this could be the worker who seeks promotion at all cost, including to others; or the gossip who trashes another's reputation in order to be liked; or the spouse who uses their strength or their words to manipulate their partner.

So this is happening all around us—and sometimes even includes us. If we have not looked at our world and cried out verse 1, then perhaps we have grown too complacent about exploitation and suffering, or maybe we have even become complicit in it.

Pray

Ask God to give you eyes to see, and a heart to feel the force of the everyday wickedness of this world.

Lift up your hand!

Read Psalm 10:12-18

❓ *What does the writer ask God to do (v 12, 15—"break the arm" means "break the power")?*

❓ *What is the writer confident about when it comes to God (v 14, 16-18)?*

As in Psalm 8, there is a mismatch between what God says and what we see—this time, between God's claim to care for the oppressed and the reality that the oppressed do not look very cared for. And there is no resolution in this psalm—the situation is described in Psalm 10:2-11, the prayer is made and the truths about God rehearsed in v 12-18, and then—the psalm ends! This is because the psalm reflects real life. When we see or are subjected to wickedness, and we ask God for help, we do not regularly witness a lightning bolt extinguishing the wicked. No, we cry out, we remind ourselves of who God is—and we wait. But as Christians now, we can wait with even greater confidence than the writer of Psalm 10...

Read Acts 17:31

❓ *How do we know God really does see, really does care, and really will judge?*

Pray

God's future judgment prevents us from despairing, or from seeking vengeance.

Thank God for his future judgment, guaranteed by Jesus' historical resurrection. Pray that you would live in light of it—realistic about this world, but not hopeless about it.

A fragrant offering

This closing section reminds us of the warmth and partnership in the gospel that Paul enjoyed with the Philippians; and what we enjoy in the gospel as Christians.

Paul's gratitude

Read Philippians 4:14-19

❓ *What is Paul grateful to the Philippians for (v 14-16, see also v 10)?*

"Share" (v 14) and "shared" (v 15) both mean "partnered".

❓ *What does Paul most desire when it comes to how the Philippians use their finances (v 17)?*

When someone invests in a business venture, they are allowed to share in the profits earned. Paul uses this metaphor to describe how this church's' financial support for his gospel work is also profiting them. By their monetary gifts, the Philippians are storing up eternal profit for themselves in heaven.

❓ *How else does Paul describe the gifts the Philippians had sent him (end v 18)?*

❓ *How should the last three words of verse 18 motivate us to use our money as the Philippians used theirs?*

❓ *How does the promise of verse 19 free us to use our money in this way?*

✔ Apply

❓ *What will taking such a view of your money mean for you practically?*

God's glory

Read Philippians 4:20-23

Verse 20 serves as a concluding doxology—word of praise—in response to all that Paul has written in this letter. Throughout the course of this epistle, Paul has taught the extraordinary truths of the saving grace of God. Each chapter has been packed with triumphant teaching that has magnified the greatness of God, including his grace that is persevering (1:6), faith-granting (1:29), sanctifying (2:12-13), justifying (3:9), empowering (3:10), glorifying (3:21), and comforting (4:5-7). The God of such abounding grace must be ascribed the glory due to his name as his people rejoice in all that he has done, is doing and will do for them.

✔ Apply

❓ *If you had to sum up the message of the letter to the Philippians in a single sentence, what would you say?*

❓ *How has your time studying Philippians...*
- *caused you to praise God?*
- *moved you to love Christ?*
- *helped you rejoice in hard circumstances?*
- *motivated you to use your words and your money to advance the gospel?*

⌃ Pray

Use your answers to the apply section above to praise God and pray to him now.

EZEKIEL: Do not mourn

We are back in Ezekiel, having covered the first 23 chapters in the last issue of Explore.

The headline so far: speaking to exiled Israelites in Babylon, God is explaining that Jerusalem is facing deserved destruction because of the people's idolatry; and yet there is some glimmer of hope and a future for God's people.

Read Ezekiel 24:1-27

This chapter comes in three parts: v 1-14, where the symbol of a boiling pot represents God's judgment against Jerusalem; v 15-18, shifting to personal information about the death of Ezekiel's wife; and v 19-27, where we discover that her death will teach the people more about the temple's destruction.

A scalded pot

- ❓ *What is significant about the date (v 1-2)?*
- ❓ *Despite containing the choice pieces of meat (v 3-5), what is the problem with the pot in God's parable (v 11-12)?*
- ❓ *What does this un-removed deposit represent (v 13)?*

The bloody meat represents corruption because it points to the violent bloodshed of this "bloody city". This image is based on Leviticus 17:10–16. Like blood poured on a bare rock and not covered with dirt, Jerusalem has done nothing to properly cover her sins, as required in Leviticus 17:13. This brings God's judgment (Ezekiel 24:14).

⌄ Apply

Judah thought of themselves as secure—here, God has a very different view of them.

- ❓ *What false grounds of eternal security do people trust in today?*
- ❓ *Which are most attractive to you?*

A horrendous event

- ❓ *What is God going to do (v 16)? How must Ezekiel respond (v 16-18)?*

This is deliberately shocking. Of course Ezekiel would want to grieve. But, with amazing trust and obedience, "I did as I had been commanded" (v 18).

- ❓ *What point is God making through Ezekiel's non-mourning (v 21-24)?*

The death of the city was truly sad. But the people were commanded not to grieve, because the judgment was right.

⌃ Pray

Ezekiel's wife was "the delight of [his] eyes" (v 16). Yet he loved God even more. So he was able to obey God even when his wife died.

Thank God that he is more worthy of adoration than even your family. Thank him that he will always be with you. Ask him to give you Ezekiel's perspective (that is a hard thing to pray).

God is not mocked

So far, Ezekiel's prophecy has focused on the judgment coming to God's people, Israel. Now, he turns to the nations who are mocking Israel in her hour of destruction.

Celebration ruined

Read Ezekiel 25:1-11

The Ammonites were known for their idolatry, cruelty and pride. (If you have time, read 1 Kings 11:7, 33; Zephaniah 2:9-10.) Their opposition to Israel is noted in Deuteronomy 23:3-4 and 1 Samuel 11:1-3.

When Israel first approached the land God had promised them, the Moabites encouraged them to worship the false god Baal (Numbers 21:1 – 25:5).

- ❓ *What had they done that had so angered God (Ezekiel 25:3, 8)?*
- ❓ *What would be their judgment (v 4-6, 9-11)?*
- ❓ *What would they know (v 11)?*

⌄ Apply

These people were so busy enjoying someone else's judgment and downfall that they never paused to look closer to home, at their own sins and their own future.

- ❓ *How do you respond to the deserved downfall of someone else?*
- ❓ *What will you think next time a criminal is rightly jailed or a fraudster is deservedly unmasked?*

···· **TIME OUT** ·····································

The world will encourage us to mock God and his righteousness.

Read Galatians 6:7-10

- ❓ *What is the right response?*

···

Read Ezekiel 25:12-17

The Edomites were descendants of Esau (Genesis 25:25, 30). They were a warring, idolatrous, proud, cruel, vengeful people (e.g. Amos 1:11).

The Philistines were a seafaring people who sought to gain control of the region. From the time of the judges they had been enemies of Israel.

- ❓ *What did Edom and Philistia do to Judah; and what was their motivation (Ezekiel 25:12, 15)?*
- ❓ *What did they get in return (v 13-14, 16-17)?*

⌃ Pray

It is wonderfully liberating to know that God says: "It is mine to avenge; I will repay" (quoted in Romans 12:19). It is also challenging; it means we must not seek our own revenge, and "if your enemy is hungry, feed him" (v 20).

Thank God that he will bring justice. Pray that you would not seek revenge, but instead would love those who treat you unfairly. Talk to God about any particular people who you are struggling to love in this way.

Seduced and destroyed

Like all idols, the love and worship of money leads to destruction.

Tyre was the commercial centre of the ancient Middle East. It was the capital of Phoenicia, which also included Sidon (see 28:21) and Byblos ("Gebal", 27:9). These were all ports.

In Ezekiel 26 – 27, Tyre comes under the scrutiny of the divine Accountant. As we'll see, Tyre had lived for money, and abused Israel in pursuit of further riches.

Seduced by riches

Read Ezekiel 26:1-18; 27:1-7

- ❷ *What did Tyre say of Jerusalem, and what opportunity did it see for itself (26:2)?*
- ❷ *What were the attractive features of its kingdom (26:11-18; 27:1-7)?*

Read Isaiah 23:15-17 (a description of Tyre), then read Revelation 18:3

- ❷ *Why is Tyre's beauty spiritually dangerous?*

Apply

Tyre represents the empty promises of riches and the depravity to which people will go in order to get them. The problem is not riches, but rather our hearts' attachment to them. And it's far easier to see this idol in others' lives than in our own.

- ❷ *How are you being tempted to love money (in having, spending, or saving it)?*

Destroyed by riches

Read Ezekiel 26:19-21; 27:25-36

- ❷ *How was rich Tyre arrogant (27:3)?*
- ❷ *How does Ezekiel speak of their fate spiritually (26:19-21)?*
- ❷ *What will happen to the wealth and reputation of Tyre (27:25-36)?*

In 26:20, the phrase "the pit" has the same meaning as the Hebrew word "Sheol": the realm of the dead. It is associated with being lost and hopeless, a place of no return. Tyre's judgment pre-figures God's final judgment upon the world. There will be no salvation for those who trust in riches.

···· **TIME OUT** ································

Read Philippians 2:3-11

How does the way of Christ, and his followers, contrast with the way of Tyre?

Pray

Thank God that Christ became poor so that through faith in him we could enjoy his eternal riches. Thank God that you do not need to chase worldly wealth. Ask God to show you where you are loving material things too much; and where you are mistreating others in the pursuit of possessions.

You're like Satan

Self-worship is rooted in pride. It believes the lie that "I" am the centre of this universe.

Ezekiel rebukes the king of Tyre in this sin—and poetically connects him to Satan, who exalted himself above God. There can be few messages more harrowing than to hear that you are like the evil one.

The foolishness of pride

Read Ezekiel 28:1-6

❓ *How does this king see himself (v 2, 6)?*

❓ *What does Ezekiel identify as the source of this pride (v 2, 5)?*

❓ *Why is it absurd for him to view himself in these ways?*

⊻ Apply

This king lived as if he was the centre of the universe.

❓ *Are there ways in which you do this? To help you work it through, think about...*
- *what drives you when you're impatient with someone else.*
- *what your priorities are today.*
- *why you ignore God's commands sometimes.*

❓ *For each of those ways, what would it look like for you to remember that God is more important than you are?*

The person of pride

Read Ezekiel 28:11-19

❓ *What do we learn about Satan in v 11-17?*

❓ *What will become of him (v 18-19)?*

These verses are a little confusing, in that they are about both the devil and the king of Tyre—sometimes more about one, other times more about the other. But the point is that the king of Tyre is being told he has a satanic attitude; and that his fall will be a shadow of Satan's.

Ezekiel refers to him as a cherub (i.e. angel) who was once in the presence of God in great splendour, and then because of his pride was cast down to the world, and made a spectacle for all the nations to see in defeat.

···· TIME OUT ·······················

Satan, like the king of Tyre, seeks worship as a god (Luke 4:6-8). He has appeared as an angel of God (2 Corinthians 11:14). And he will one day be judged (Revelation 20:10).

The end of pride

Read Ezekiel 28:6-10, 20-26

❓ *What reversals take place in verses 6-10?*

❓ *What does God promise for his people in the future (v 24-26)?*

⌃ Pray

Pride is self-dependent. True faith is utterly Christ-dependent. So confess now that there is nothing in you that deserves eternal life; and thank God for giving you life in Christ, and gifts and opportunities to serve him.

Bible in a year: Job 4 – 7

From monster to carcass

Israel's plan to be a great nation, not needing to rely on God, had backfired on them when Egypt betrayed them in their hour of need. God would judge them both.

God will judge us for rejecting him and will judge the world for aiding in that sin.

The boastful beast

Read Ezekiel 29:1-7

(If you have time, read to verse 20.)

❷ *What does God compare Pharaoh to? What does he rebuke him for (v 1-3)?*

The word "monster" can also mean "crocodile". Crocodiles were caught by hooks and pulled onto land for slaughter. Pharaoh was thought to be divine, and so was the crocodile.

❷ *What is going to happen to Pharaoh (v 1-5)?*

❷ *With what does God compare Pharaoh's help to Israel (v 6-7)?*

⌄ Apply

To all the world, an alliance with Egypt looked like a sensible, secure option for Israel. But the world was wrong.

❷ *Where does the world tell you to put your security?*

❷ *How might God disagree with options the world sees as sensible?*

The destructive day

Read Ezekiel 29:21 – 30:19

❷ *What day is coming (30:1-3)?*

❷ *What will happen to Egypt's...*
  • *wealth (30:1-4)?*
  • *lands (30:8-19)?*

The "day of the LORD" describes the day at the end of all time, when God will come to judge the world (e.g. Isaiah 2:12, 17).

❷ *What hope does God offer Israel for that day (Ezekiel 29:21)?*

The "horn" is a symbol of strength (see 1 Samuel 2:1; 1 Kings 22:11). Here, it means the rise of a leader of unusual strength and power. The word "grow" is a specific messianic term. It means a "sprout" or "shoot" of new growth. It's pointing us to Christ, the one who enables us to know God, and to be in relationship with God, looking forward to eternity with God. God is warning through Ezekiel that the day is coming when even the strongest will be destroyed; and when the only hope will be to look to the "horn" he has raised up.

⌃ Pray

Praise God that there will be justice in this world on those who oppose him and his people; and salvation on that day for those who look to his "horn", the Lord Jesus. Ask God to give you a greater confidence in his justice, joy in his salvation, and motivation to speak about his Christ.

Biblical realism

Here is a psalm for our times. It tells us how to think and what to do when God is ignored, faith is mocked, and biblical ethics are unpopular.

Retreat

Read Psalm 11:1-3

King David seems to be facing opposition and the very real danger of defeat.

❷ *What are his advisors saying to him (v 1-3)?*

We hear this—and perhaps feel this—all the time. Western nations are, by and large, turning further and further from biblical morality, and turning more and more aggressive towards Bible-believers. What is left to do but retreat into our church buildings, close the doors, hope society will ignore us, and leave the world to itself? After all, it is very dangerous out there.

That's the advice David is getting. But it's not advice that David will be taking...

Stand firm

Read Psalm 11:4-7

David does not look around, so much as up and forwards.

❷ *What is true about God, at that very moment (v 4)?*

❷ *What is God doing, at that very moment (v 4-5)?*

❷ *What will God do, one day (v 6)?*

❷ *What does God hate, and what does God love?*

God's eyes see everything. He sees the rejecting of him and the mockery or worse against his people. And he will judge it. And he also sees those who stand upright—not running from the world, but standing firm in the world. He will ensure that those people "will see his face". His people are not to retreat—we are to advance, on towards the day when justice is done and we see our Saviour face to face.

David won't give in to defeatist pessimism—but nor does he resort to complacent optimism. Instead, he lives with biblical realism. God is still on his heavenly throne, whatever the world thinks or wishes. God will bring justice, no matter how much the wicked dispute what justice is or whether God should bring it. God will bring his people through to his presence, despite the arrows fired at the faithful throughout their lives. This is reality—so David will not, and we must not, retreat or give up.

⌄ Apply

❷ *How does this psalm encourage you to keep going and stay public, as a Christian?*

❷ *How will remembering that God is "on his heavenly throne" change the way you live this week?*

Tall tree, big fall

Today's headline is: everyone and every nation that exalts itself above God will be brought low on the day of the Lord.

So today's application is: we should humble ourselves and live in light of his majesty.

Deserved judgment

Read Ezekiel 31:1-14; 32:9-16

- ❓ *Which nation does God compare Egypt to (31:1-9)?*
- ❓ *How is God going to deal with them (32:11-16)?*
- ❓ *Who will be used to make this happen (32:11)?*

Often in Scripture, Egypt represents the whole idea of trusting in the world instead of in God. The image of the birds settling and finding shade in Assyria's tree (31:6) is the picture of the nations finding their security and hope in Egypt.

Read Ezekiel 17:23

God had already spoken of a greater tree, raised up by him, to provide true shade for all people. Egypt is an inferior rival to God's plans.

···· **TIME OUT** ·································

It's helpful for us to remember that in every age, there are different "trees" on offer—places to seek rest, and shade, and security. Only one—God's—truly offers those things.

- ❓ *What alternatives are promoted by your society, and by your heart?*

Defenceless against judgment

Read Ezekiel 30:20-26; 32:1-8

- ❓ *What will happen to Pharaoh's strength? What will happen to the king of Babylon's strength (30:21-25)?*
- ❓ *What will happen to the Egyptians (30:26)?*
- ❓ *What will happen around Egypt in the time of their judgment (32:3-8)?*

···· **TIME OUT** ·································

God is utterly sovereign over even the most powerful state; he determines its rise and fall.

- ❓ *How should this shape our view of our world, and our own country, today?*

Doomed in judgment

How will people look at Egypt once its judgment has come (32:9-10)? Egypt has never again been a true world power. Their former glory is a reminder of God's control of his world, and his judgment in the course of history.

⌃ Pray

How should we feel about this passage? Grateful that God is in control; sorrowful at the state of our world. Express both to God in prayer. Pray for any you know who believe they have found safety in a worldly "tree".

Warning

Chapters 25 – 32 were about the judgment of the nations. The next five chapters (33 – 37) return to the earlier theme of the fall of Jerusalem to the Babylonians.

Ezekiel will remind his hearers of their personal responsibility to respond to God by repenting of false assumptions of self-righteousness.

Clear warning

Read Ezekiel 33:1-20

- ❷ *What is the watchman to do and what is he responsible for here (v 1-6)?*
- ❷ *How does that job apply to Ezekiel (v 7-8)?*
- ❷ *What is his message (v 10-16)?*
- ❷ *What ideas does he need to oppose (v 17-18)?*

This chapter parallels Ezekiel 3:16-21, where Ezekiel was first appointed watchman over Israel. Watchmen were placed in towers on the walls of the ancient cities (e.g. Isaiah 21:6). The "trumpet" (Ezekiel 33:3) was a "shofar", or ram's horn, that was used to sound the warning of an approaching enemy.

The point is that God's judgment is coming, and everyone needs to know that they are sinners, they have made themselves his enemies, and they cannot hope to stand successfully against him.

···· TIME OUT ·························

A watchman's message ("The enemy is coming!") will never be popular; but it is always vital.

❷ *How does this help us have realistic expectations, and renewed motivation, about warning people they're sinful, and that they face God's judgment?*

Plain meaning

Read Ezekiel 33:21-33

- ❷ *What enables Ezekiel to speak freely (v 21-22)?*
- ❷ *What faulty logic are the people relying on (v 24)?*

God's point in verses 23-29 is: *You are not like Abraham. He trusted and sought to obey me: you don't.*

- ❷ *What is tragic about Ezekiel's audience (v 30-33)?*

☑ Apply

❷ *Are there any ways in which verse 31 is true of you? What will you do about it?*

Although the world may reject our message of warning now, one day it will see that we were right (v 33). The challenge is to speak the truth now, before the whole world sees, too late, that it is the truth.

☑ Apply

Is there anyone you're not warning because you're worried about what they'll think or say of you?

Call yourself a shepherd?

The way people use authority should reflect how God uses his; but more often, it reflects our own sinfulness. The news is full of examples of authority being abused.

God's people, ever since the time of David, had been promised a great king, who would shepherd his people wisely and well (2 Samuel 7). God called his people's leaders to act as their shepherds in every generation. But...

The rebuke

Read Ezekiel 34:1-6

- ❷ *Who do these shepherds care for (v 2)?*
- ❷ *What have they done, and not done (v 3-4)?*
- ❷ *What has not marked their care and how have they ruled (v 4)?*
- ❷ *What result has this had on the "flock" of Israel (v 5-6)?*

"Shepherd" was a common metaphor for "king" in the Old Testament (e.g. Isaiah 44:28; Jeremiah 10:21). The shepherd provided care, leadership and protection. So should the king and leaders of Israel.

Apply

Think about any areas of life where you have authority (in the home, at work, in the community, and so on).

- ❷ *Are your actions motivated by a desire for your own power or comfort, or the care of others?*

···**TIME OUT**···

Read 1 Peter 5:1-4

- ❷ *In what sense are church pastors "shepherds"?*
- ❷ *What kind of shepherds are they to be?*

Pray for your own church's pastors and elders now.

The account

Read Ezekiel 34:7-10

- ❷ *Why are God's words to his shepherds in verse 10 both surprising and justified?*
- ❷ *What will God do for the flock?*

The lesson is plain. A lack of godly leadership leads to the downfall of God's people. As the leader goes, so do the people—for better or for worse.

Pray

Read John 10:11-18

- ❷ *In what ways is Jesus a "good" shepherd?*
- ❷ *How does reading Ezekiel 34:1-10 help you to appreciate and praise him even more?*

Do so now!

The sheep and the pasture

What does caring leadership look like for God's people?

Here, God declares that one day his people will be perfectly cared for—because they'll be cared for by him.

Read Ezekiel 34:11-31

Search and rescue

Ezekiel points his listeners to the future as he continues to speak symbolically of the relationship of God and his people in terms of a shepherd and sheep.

- ❓ *What do the sheep need God to do for them (v 12)?*
- ❓ *What promise is made to the sheep (v 13-14)?*

Chosen sheep

- ❓ *What kind of sheep does God rescue? What kind of sheep don't get saved (v 16, 20)?*
- ❓ *Look at verse 21. What are the larger, fatter sheep using their strength to do?*

This is a picture of people who live for themselves, using what they have to get more. It's an accurate picture of almost every king of Israel since David and Solomon!

···· TIME OUT ····

Read Matthew 25:31-33

In the Middle East, sheep and goats are virtually indistinguishable from each other.

But Jesus can judge between people—and how someone treats those who are weaker than themselves is the outward sign that he will judge.

Secure sheep

- ❓ *What royal figure will be "prince" over these sheep (Ezekiel 34:24)?*

This passage is not saying David himself will return, resurrected, to rule over Israel. Ezekiel is speaking of the return of one like David, descended from David. One who, like David, will triumph against all his foes, extend his kingdom, and unite God's people.

- ❓ *What covenant (i.e. binding agreement) will God make (v 25)?*
- ❓ *What will happen, and what won't happen, in this pasture (v 26-31)?*

Ezekiel leaves us searching for a son of David who will fulfil this wonderful picture. It's why the pulse quickens when we're told that Jesus is "the son of David" (Matthew 1:1); and why blind Bartimaeus knows that Jesus, the "son of David", will have mercy on him (Mark 10:47).

🔺 Pray

Spend time simply praising Jesus for who he is: your King and your Shepherd.

Two mountains, two ways

It's sometimes said that as there are many paths up a mountain, there are many routes to God. God says something very different.

There are many mountains, and only one of them leads to life with him.

Contemptible sayings

Read Ezekiel 35:1-15

❷ *What mountain is in view here (v 2-3)?*

❷ *What will God do to those who live on it (v 2-4, 6-9)?*

❷ *Why?*

- *v 5*
- *v 10, 12*
- *v 13*

Mount Seir is identified with Edom (v 15), Israel's ancient enemy. It is used to represent the opposite of the kingdom we'll see portrayed in Ezekiel 36. It is a kingdom set against God.

···· TIME OUT ·····································

❷ *What do the various attitudes we see in Edom look like in the modern world around you?*

Reflective sayings

Read Ezekiel 36:1-21

❷ *Which mountain range is now in view (v 1)?*

And the people living here are the object of scorn from those around them (v 1-6).

❷ *So what does God promise (v 7)?*

❷ *What is God going to do for Israel (v 8-12)?*

❷ *How is this different from where Israel's own efforts had brought her (v 16-19)?*

The two mountain ranges represent two very different ways to live, or paths to take. And they lead to two very different destinations. We all live on one mountainside or the other, and face one future or the other.

☑ Apply

❷ *Where do you live?*

❷ *How is your life reflecting the way of life of people on that mountain?*

❷ *If you are a member of God's people, are there any ways you are living as though you were a resident of Mount Seir?*

◭ Pray

Pray that the world's empty promises and boasts would grow dim, and that God's promises to you in Christ would be all you listen to. Speak to God about any ways the world seems particularly attractive to you at the moment.

Heart surgery

God isn't simply promising to restore his people to former glories. He's telling them that they will be raised to a glorious status that has never been seen before.

Purpose

Read Ezekiel 36:22-23

God is about to make some amazing promises. But for whose sake is he going to do these things for Israel (v 22)?

The worst thing about God's people being defeated, exiled and scattered is not them being mocked; it's God being mocked—his name being "profaned" (v 22-23). His reputation is at stake: can he keep his promises to bless his people?

So God saves sinners for his own glory. We are not at the centre of his plans: he is. He is perfect, and in saving his people he is seen to be perfect; his reputation is upheld. Our greatest good is to be part of his purposes to bring himself glory.

···· TIME OUT ····································

Read Ephesians 1:3-14

❷ *What has God done for us through Christ? How does this make you feel?*

❷ *What is the purpose of all he has done (v 6, 12, 14)?*

People

Read Ezekiel 36:24-27

❷ *What is God going to do for his people (v 24-25)?*

❷ *What "surgery" is going to be performed, and why (v 26-27)?*

God's image was placed in humanity to reflect God's character as they ruled the world (Genesis 1 – 2). But humanity failed; the image of God was spoiled by sin. So he called Israel to show God's goodness to the nations (Exodus 19:6; Deuteronomy 4:6); but Israel failed too, as we've seen in Ezekiel. Now there will be a new Israel, called by God to enjoy living with and for him; and, crucially, to have new, Spirit-filled hearts, which want to—and are able to—keep God's laws.

⯆ Apply

Just like every other spiritual blessing, a Spirit-filled heart comes through faith in Christ (John 3:5-15).

❷ *Does your walk match your talk? In what ways do you need to ask the Spirit to move you to obey God?*

Place

Read Ezekiel 36:28-38

❷ *How would you summarise the kind of place God will bring his people into?*

Notice Ezekiel refers to this promised place being "like the garden of Eden" (v 35). Ultimately, he's pointing us to the recreated Eden, the new creation. Praise God now for the land he is leading you to.

Words

Words—we use, on average, around 13,000 of them each day. They're used to praise and criticise, to love and to hurt, to build up and to tear down.

Their words

Read Psalm 12:1-4

David's living at a time and in a place where it seems the "faithful" have "vanished". Perhaps that's a place you know all too well—at work, or in the family home, or at a restaurant with friends.

❷ *In this ungodly situation, what does David notice about how people use their words (v 2, 4)?*

❷ *Who is in charge of their mouths? Whose cause do they want to advance with their words (v 4)?*

···· TIME OUT ·······································

❷ *How do you see words being used to lie, flatter, deceive and self-promote around you?*

❷ *Do you ever notice yourself doing one or more of these things with what you say?*

His words

Read Psalm 12:5-8

❷ *Who speaks in verse 5? What is being promised?*

In the Psalms, this is the first time we have heard God's voice since Psalm 2:6-9—and, as there, these are words of judgment. The ungodly use their words to oppress those who can't defend themselves (12:2, 4), and prompt groaning among those who are

deceived or triumphed over. And God will not let that go unjudged.

❷ *David's living in a world of lies. What do we discover that's different about the words of the Lord in verse 6?*

Apply

❷ *Why is verse 6 great news?*

❷ *Whose words are you more affected by: God's, or the world's?*

❷ *Whose words do you repeat more often: what you've heard others say or what you've heard God say?*

Our words

Read Acts 2:1-8, 14-24

When the Holy Spirit comes into Jesus' followers, the first thing he transforms is their speech (v 4).

❷ *What does he enable them to do (v 8)?*

❷ *So they can speak about what (v 22-24)?*

❷ *So what should Jesus' Spirit-filled people today be using our words to do?*

Pray

Thank God for his flawless, precious words in Scripture. Confess any ways in which your words have been like those of Psalm 12:2, 4. Ask God to give you words which point others to the life, death, resurrection and reign of Jesus Christ.

Bone operation

Remember, Ezekiel is speaking to exiles: members of Israel who are cut off from God's land, far from God's temple, away from God's blessings.

Spiritually speaking, they are as good as dead.

From death…

Read Ezekiel 37:1-6

❷ *Where does God lead Ezekiel (v 1-2)?*

❷ *What is the natural answer to God's question in verse 3? How does Ezekiel answer (v 3)?*

❷ *What is the real answer (v 5-6)?*

Here is the picture. Israel was dead. Their special call to be a light to the nations seemed lost. How could God reverse the effects of their sin? He would have to recreate them.

This vision shows us that Israel's deepest problem is not exile but death. God's people must be delivered from death in order to enter the land of life. So this picture of the valley of death is a picture of anyone, spiritually, who is a sinner.

···· TIME OUT ·····································

Read Ephesians 2:1-3

❷ *How do Paul's stark words here pick up on the truths of Ezekiel's valley of death?*

❷ *When, and why, are we tempted to ignore or downplay these truths?*

… to life

Read Ezekiel 37:7-14

❷ *What began to happen after Ezekiel prophesied in the vision (v 7-8)?*

❷ *What else does Ezekiel prophesy (v 9-10)?*

❷ *What is the vision meant to teach the exiles (v 11-14)?*

This image of God's creative power is similar to the creation of Adam in Genesis 2:7. God gives life, through his word; as his messenger speaks, bones become beings.

···· TIME OUT ·····································

Read Ephesians 2:4-10

❷ *How do Paul's wonderful words here pick up on the truths of Ezekiel's valley of new life?*

✔ Apply

❷ *What difference would it make to your feelings, actions and prayers today if you remembered…*
  • *the fact of the valley of death?*
  • *the hope of the valley of life?*

▲ Pray

Thank God for bringing you from spiritual death to eternal life, through Christ. Thank God for the future he has given you. Ask God to give you greater confidence in his life-giving word.

Two become one

God's people have been scattered and exiled. How will they ever be united under his rule and live in the land of God's blessing again?

This section speaks directly to this; but (as we'll see) the fulfilment of this vision is greater than Ezekiel's hearers could ever have imagined.

Gathering exiles

Read Ezekiel 37:15-23

- ❷ *What is Ezekiel told to do with the sticks (v 15-17)?*
- ❷ *What does this action mean (v 18-22)?*
- ❷ *What does God promise will never happen again (v 23)?*

The strongest sons of Jacob, the father of Israel, were Judah and Joseph. Those two names are used here to represent the once-divided kingdom.

God declares that in the promised restoration there will no longer be two kingdoms, but one. That means hope for scattered exiles! In the New Testament, those who are trusting God by faith in Christ are referred to as exiles (e.g. 1 Peter 1:1, ESV), scattered across the world. It is to those people that Christ promises to "send out the angels and gather his elect from the four winds, from the ends of the earth" (Mark 13:27).

- ❷ *So why is Ezekiel's vision precious for us today?*

Blessing exiles

Read Ezekiel 37:24-28

And now God tells us what life in this new, restored, united kingdom will be like.

- ❷ *Who will be king, and how will the people respond to his rule and laws (v 24)?*
- ❷ *Who will be there, and for how long (v 25)?*
- ❷ *Why is this certain, even though it still lies in the future (v 26)?*
- ❷ *What will be God's relationship to this place and people (v 27)?*

Notice that while this will be good for God's people, supremely it is being done so that all people will recognise God as God, as he deserves (v 28).

Again, we know "my servant David" (v 24) points to David's greater son, Jesus Christ (Matthew 1:1). It is the covenant promise that he makes through his death (Luke 22:19-20) that is the one being promised here.

❤ Apply

Read James 1:1-5

- ❷ *What is one application of being a member of the "scattered" people of God in this world?*
- ❷ *Is this your view of the trials you face on your way to God's perfect land?*

Bible in a year: Job 32 – 34 • Psalm 62

Who opposes you?

It is far better to be opposed by the world today than by God eternally. It is far better to be loved by God eternally than by the world today.

This section of Ezekiel is picturing the "ideal Israel"—an Israel whom God is recreating and gathering from all over the world.

In this part of that vision, these people have the four corners of the earth against them. The good news is that God is no longer against them.

The world against God

Read Ezekiel 38:1-13

❷ *What coalition does Gog command (v 4-6)?*

❷ *Who is actually in control, though (v 4)?*

❷ *What is their evil plot against Israel (v 10-13)?*

"Gog" and "Magog" are being used as symbols of an enemy to come—whoever it might be, and from whatever region. These titles are used here symbolically of the final whole-world uprising against Jerusalem, its people and king.

This vision is filled out in the New Testament. Revelation 16:12-14 speaks of Babylon gathering all nations against God and his people. The battle will peak with Satan leading Gog, to revolt against God (Revelation 20:7-8). This attack comes not just from the north, but the four corners of the world. Before full restoration, God's people will know formidable persecution.

Apply

We see here that evil is never out of God's control, nor can it frustrate his purposes.

❷ *How does this encourage you today?*

God against the world

Read Ezekiel 38:14-22 (if you have time, read to 39:29)

❷ *What will happen to Gog (38:19-22)?*

❷ *Why do you think there is so much detail given? What does God want us to understand?*

Apply

Read Colossians 1:21-23

❷ *How does Ezekiel 38 help you understand the seriousness of being "alienated from God ... enemies"?*

❷ *How does Ezekiel 38 help you appreciate Christ's death, which has brought you friendship with God?*

❷ *How does Ezekiel 38 motivate you to "continue in your faith"—whatever the world thinks about you doing that?*

Pray

Thank God that through faith you are no longer an enemy but a friend. Talk to God about the times in your life when you need courage and conviction to live by faith.

The temple of God's glory

Today, we're covering six chapters—and they're six of the most difficult in the Bible. But they're best grasped from a big-picture view, instead of a microscopic one.

Three things to help guide you:

- The temple in the Old Testament always pointed to God's presence, where you could worship him and atone for sins by offering sacrifices.

- Ezekiel's temple vision communicates that God's people will be restored to true worship, and his presence will be central to their lives for ever.

- In this vision, God is bringing sinners into his presence through a temple not made with human hands.

Read Ezekiel 40:1-4; 43:1-27

A city on a mountain

❓ *What is the context of this vision (40:2)?*

The city vision folds into the temple vision.

❓ *What is the most exciting event that takes place in this temple (43:1-5)?*

❓ *How does this differ from 10:1-18?*

The temple represents the heavenly throne. The interior of the temple (41:25), is adorned with carvings of cherubim. The palm trees (v 25-26) are perhaps recalling a refreshing, Eden-like oasis.

❓ *Why would this vision of God's glory returning be encouraging to a people who were suffering and in exile?*

Ultimately, God is pointing to a human temple: a man in whom "we have seen his glory, the glory of the one and only Son,

who came from the Father" (John 1:14). Jesus Christ is the true temple; the former temple was symbolic. By coming to Jesus as King and Saviour, we come to God; we worship God; and we are forgiven by God. (If you have time, read Hebrews 10:1-14.)

A perfect temple

Much of these chapters are taken up with measurements! The point is that this is God's perfect, ordered, sovereign plan for his forgiven people, living in his place, with him present among them. Everything is precisely as he wills it.

We find the same focus on measurements at the end of Revelation. God's new creation—the ultimate temple of his presence—is perfect. And today, believers are the first part of this new-creation-temple-building (Ephesians 2:19-21).

So, putting it all together, Jesus is the temple; he is building his people into this God-dwelling structure; and one day, the whole new creation will be this perfect temple of God's presence.

⌃ Pray

Praise God for what he has done in Christ; what he is doing in and through his people; and what he will do in this world when he remakes it. Praise him for making you part of this eternal plan!

The Lord is there

As Ezekiel finishes his prophecy, he continues to focus on God's future temple.

River of life

Read Ezekiel 47:1-12

❷ *What does Ezekiel see coming from the south side of the temple (v 1-2)?*

❷ *What happens to this stream through v 1-5?*

❷ *What is the effect of this river (v 7-12)?*

This river has life-giving properties. Whatever the water touches is given life (v 9); and it is life that never fails or fades (v 12).

···· TIME OUT ···

Read John 7:37-39

❷ *How does Ezekiel 47 make Jesus' words here wonderfully exciting?*

❷ *In what sense have Christians already begun to enjoy eternal life?*

In his Gospel, John (alone of the Gospel writers) chose to mention the "sudden flow of blood and water" (John 19:34) that came from Jesus as his side was pierced on the cross. Perhaps John wants us to join the dots and understand that it is from the cross of Christ that the river of salvation-life flows.

A message for then

Read Ezekiel 47:13 – 48:35

❷ *How is the land divided (47:14)?*

❷ *How are non-Israelites ("aliens/ foreigners") to be treated (v 21-23)?*

❷ *What is the name of this city (48:35)?*

Ezekiel lives among a group of people who have been exiled from the land, scattered among the nations, and are far from God and his blessings. God has explained to them why this is happening (his right judgment on their sin). So how precious these promises must have been to them! How wonderful to know that they would one day live in God's land; that members of the nations would join them; that they would live in a place where the Lord was.

A message for us today

Ezekiel is a word for us, too. Because of our sin, we are all naturally not God's people, not able to live in God's presence (1 Peter 2:10). And yet in Christ we are brought in. We can enjoy now, and look forward to enjoying fully, living as part of God's people gathered from every nation, in the presence of God himself. We can know that one day we will live in a place of which we can say: "The Lord is there". **Read Revelation 22:1-6.**

⌃ Pray

Praise God that sin is not the end of the story; that being scattered is not the end of the story; that living in his presence as his people is our eternal story. Thank God for what Ezekiel has taught you about God, yourself, and the future.

MARK: A struggle for sight

We rejoin Jesus and his disciples in Mark 8 on their journey to Jerusalem. It begins and ends with healing a blind man, but the stories in between are about spiritual blindness.

Read Mark 8:22-26

One detail of the story stands out right away that troubles many people. Why did it take Jesus two attempts to heal this man's blindness? Did Jesus make a mistake or do something wrong the first time? No! The answer is quite simple: this healing is a parable.

Seeing clearly

Read Mark 8:27-33

❷ *Looking just at verses 27-29, do you think Peter sees Jesus clearly?*

❷ *What about when you add in verses 31-33?*

Peter has declared that Jesus is the Messiah, but he doesn't understand what being the Messiah is all about. He still needs to have his spiritual eyes opened.

❷ *How does this link with the story in verses 22-26?*

❷ *What kind of Messiah is Jesus (v 31)?*

Less is more

Read Mark 8:34-38

Not only would Jesus die on a cross but those who followed him would also have to carry a cross. We are to embrace "the concerns of God".

❷ *What three things does Jesus tell us to do (v 34) and why (v 35)?*

The world constantly pursues getting ahead by getting more stuff—self-denial seems like the path of loss, not gain. But let's say that you are so wildly successful in your quest to say yes to yourself that you end up gaining the whole world. Is it worth it if in the process you lose your soul (v 36)?

⌄ Apply

❷ *What things do you long for that might be hindering your life in Jesus?*

❷ *What is it that you are looking to gain?*

Warning and promise

There is a warning here. Following Jesus means not being ashamed of him and his words (v 38). If we have been ashamed of him in this life, he will be ashamed of us in the life to come.

But don't miss the promise too. Jesus calls us to lose our lives for his sake (v 35). We deny lesser things to get greater things. Jesus is saying, *As you deny yourself, you find your real self and eternal life in me.*

⌃ Pray

Ask your heavenly Father to help you see both Jesus and yourself clearly and to keep your eyes fixed on the promises you have in him.

How long, O Lord?

Today's psalm is full of raw pain and emotion. Chances are that this last year you've felt like this—and that at some point in the next year, you'll feel this way again.

Read Psalm 13

How long?

- ❷ *How would you sum up how David is feeling in v 1-2, and why?*
- ❷ *Have you ever felt some of this? Did you talk to God about it? What did you say?*

Sometimes, when we are disorientated by feeling deserted, depressed or defeated, we think we must hide it from God, and pretend we are keeping calm and carrying on.

That's not what God's inspired word encourages us to do here. We're to come to the Lord, the God with whom we have a relationship, as our Father as well as our King. We're to pour out our feelings to him, and even ask him what he is doing. It is not wrong to come to God and ask, "How long, Lord"? What is wrong is not to come to him at all.

⌃ Pray

Is there an area of your life about which you've simply not been speaking to God? Will you talk to him about it now, even if all you can say is "How long?" or "Why"?

Look on me

- ❷ *What does David ask God to do (v 3-4)?*
- ❷ *How is David acknowledging his complete dependence on God?*

⌃ Pray

Are you trying to rely on yourself to get through a difficult time? Are you trying to resist the temptations of the devil on your own? Stop now, and pray to the one who can help you when you are helpless.

But I trust

David has no idea what God is doing (v 1-2); he's in sorrow and facing opposition (v 2, 4).

- ❷ *But what still brings him joy in the middle of so much pain (v 5)?*
- ❷ *What does he decide to do, even while he cries out (v 6)?*

When we ask God, "How long?" and beg him to look on us and help, we also need to remember his love and salvation and goodness to us, seen most clearly of all at the cross. **Read Romans 5:8**.

⌃ Pray

Thank God for all he has done, is doing and will do for you. Ask him to give you joy when you know sorrow, and a song when you are crying.

Perhaps you're not in a Psalm 13-type situation right now—but the chances are you one day will be. How will you ensure you remember this psalm on that future day?

The transfiguration

Jesus doesn't reflect glory—he produces it.

Read Mark 9:1-13

Three disciples go up a mountain with Jesus. What they witness is the kingdom of God coming in power (v 1). Peter, James and John get to see the divine power and glory of our Lord Jesus Christ on display. The transfiguration is the gift of sight, but Peter is blind to what he is seeing.

❓ *What is the disciples' reaction (v 6)?*

❓ *Why do you think Peter reacted as he did (v 5)?*

···· **TIME OUT** ··

Read Exodus 34:28-32

The exodus is a really important backstory for the transfiguration. But there is also a stunning difference between the two. At Sinai, Moses saw the glory of God and even reflected it in his own face, as the moon reflects the glory of the sun (Exodus 34:29). Jesus, however, is not like the moon but the sun itself—the source of the glory.

The Father speaks

The Father's words are a direct rebuke. Peter's proposal would have put Jesus on the same level as Moses and Elijah. They reflected the glory of God. Jesus *is* the glory of God. They spoke from God; Jesus speaks *as* God.

This was the one moment when Jesus' divine nature overshadowed and outshone

his human nature. It was a sneak peek at the second coming, the day when Jesus will come "in his Father's glory with the holy angels" (Mark 8:38).

⌄ Apply

❓ *How does this vision of Jesus' glory impact how you see him?*

❓ *How will it influence the way you think about his second coming?*

Still blind

Rising from the dead can only come after being dead. It is a package deal! We are back to what Jesus said in Mark 8:31—he must suffer and be killed and after three days rise again. Have the disciples learned their lesson? No. They don't understand what he means (9:10). They have missed the suffering part of the picture again!

❓ *Why do you think the disciples keep their questions to themselves this time (v 10)?*

❓ *Why might they try to change the subject (v 11)?*

❓ *How does Jesus bring it back to the point again (v 12)?*

⌃ Pray

These stories of partial blindness can serve as a spiritual check-up for us. Do these truths thrill your spiritual tastebuds? Whatever your response, bring it to Jesus.

Bible in a year: 1 Samuel 1 – 3 • Jeremiah 15

"Help my unbelief"

Bringing our doubts to Jesus does not offend him.

Read Mark 9:14-29

❷ *What were the people arguing about (v 14, 18)?*

❷ *What does the father of the child think about Jesus (v 17, 22)?"*

Partial faith

Faith recognises that there is nothing that can hold Jesus back—he is both willing and able. The father of the demon-possessed child takes Jesus' word to heart. He sees the real source of the problem: he believes partially, not fully.

What should he do about that? Try harder? Resolve to doubt less? No—he brings even his unbelief to Jesus.

❷ *How is the father's response to Jesus described (v 24)?*

Pride will often keep us from crying out in desperation. We don't want people to see us that needy. If we face difficulties, sometimes the impulse is to try harder, do better, or persevere longer. It is a symptom of the same problem—proud unbelief.

In verse 24, the father has faith that Jesus can even help him with his lack of faith. Jesus already sees what is in our hearts. He knows the problem. But have we reached the point where we will humble ourselves, confess our need, bring it to him, and beg him to do what only he can do?

❷ *Does pride ever keep you from praying?*

❷ *How does Jesus' willingness (v 23, 25) and his gentleness (v 27) encourage you to come to him today in prayer?*

⌃ Pray

Spend some time asking God for anything you may have resisted bringing before him.

Just ask

This story ends once again with a comment on the problem with the disciples. Jesus shows them that their perennial problem is their prayerlessness (v 29). They are relying on their own strength.

The father of the demon-possessed boy had partial faith and partial unbelief, and he asked for help with his unbelief. The disciples are in the same position, and they need the same solution.

⌄ Apply

❷ *What are the things that you tend to turn to instead of praying when you face difficulties? Is it thinking more, studying more or speaking to other people?*

❷ *How could you remind yourself to pray first?*

The surprising insight is that weakness and desperation is actually a gift. The only thing we really need is to feel our need for him.

Who is welcome?

A lively conversation is happening on the way to Jerusalem.

Read Mark 9:30-37

Blindness

Despite Jesus' constant teaching on his death and resurrection, the disciples fail to understand, and they are afraid to ask for help (v 32). The rest of the story is going to help us see that "afraid to ask" really means "too arrogant to ask".

> ❷ *What is Jesus trying to explain to his disciples (v 31)?*
> ❷ *Why did the disciples not answer Jesus' question (v 33-34)?*

This series of events is strikingly jarring and disorienting. What would you do if you just heard your beloved master say that he was going to die?

Their blindness flows from their delusions of grandeur. Mark explicitly says that this argument took place "on the way". He repeats the phrase (v 33, 34) so that we won't miss it. This phrase is a reference to the journey they are taking to Jerusalem. They think it is a glory road leading to exaltation. But this is the Calvary road. This journey is leading to humiliation. Suffering must precede glory. Jesus has work to do in resetting the disciples' expectations.

Correction

Jesus starts with a lesson in humility. He does not rebuke them for wanting to be great. Their endeavour to be first is not wrong—just misguided. They are using worldly categories for greatness. Jesus teaches them about his upside-down kingdom, where the way to real happiness is to seek the happiness of others.

> ❷ *What might being a "servant of all" look like (v 35)?*
> ❷ *Why do you think Jesus uses a child to reinforce his lesson (v 36-37)?*

No spiritual snobbery

A flourishing church is a place where the weak and poor and frail flourish. A place full of big hearts not big shots. We do not view people as those to evaluate and compete with but those to serve.

Jesus is more ready to receive you than you are ready to be received. Indeed, the Father's arms are open to you and the family of God is open to you only because the Son stretched out his arms for you on the cross.

☑ Apply

These words test our hearts.

> ❷ *What are the ways in which you're tempted to size people up or dismiss them if they're not important enough?*
> ❷ *What would it look like to love people without looking for anything in return?*
> ❷ *Who can you serve or welcome today?*

Bible in a year: 1 Samuel 8 – 10 • Hebrews 1

Another eye exam

How do we view others? The eye test in the next passage is really a heart test—and the disciples fail once again.

Read Mark 9:38-41

The whole scene is ironic. Jesus has barely finished teaching them that they need to receive people in his name (v 36-37) when John tells him that someone has been casting out demons "in your name" (v 38).

> ❓ *How did the disciples react to this man (v 38)?*
>
> ❓ *How is this scene doubly ironic in the light of what's recently happened (v 17-18)?*
>
> ❓ *Why do the disciples not celebrate this defeat of dark spirits?*

···· TIME OUT ···

Read Numbers 11:26-29

As God's people travelled through the wilderness on the way to the promised land, some people began to speak as prophets who were not official prophets like Moses. Joshua, who had assisted Moses since he was young, was troubled that others were speaking for the Lord.

> ❓ *How does this mirror the disciples' attitudes?*
>
> ❓ *How is Moses' response like that of Jesus?*

The heart of it

The disciples have narrow, prideful hearts that seem bent on cornering the market in ministry—but Jesus' heart is different.

> ❓ *What is the first reason Jesus gives for his command not to stop the man (v 39)?*
>
> ❓ *What is the second reason (v 40)?*

This is a war: the kingdom of God versus the kingdom of Satan. Satan and his demons are the ones "against us". There is no problem with what this person is doing or the name he is using—he simply fails to be in the disciples' company. Verse 41 tells us even the smallest act has great significance when it is done for the greatest name.

✅ Apply

Jesus' words are an assault on our pride.

> ❓ *Are there times when you are quick to exclude people and draw your circle small?*
>
> ❓ *When do you find yourself judging the supposed size of people's actions? Noticing large, sensational works, and overlooking small, everyday acts of kindness?*

🔼 Pray

Jesus came and tore down the dividing wall between us by his blood. Let this text speak to you and ask God how you can grow to be a disciple who welcomes other disciples, including those with different customs to yours. Pray that your church would be a welcoming, big-hearted, open-armed church.

Bible in a year: 1 Samuel 11 – 13 • Acts 13

The reality of hell

Today's passage makes many people uncomfortable because it speaks very directly of the doctrine of hell—but this doctrine doesn't embarrass Jesus.

Read Mark 9:42-50

Metaphor

The word that Jesus uses for "hell" is the Greek word Gehenna. Gehenna was a valley to the southwest of Jerusalem. It was a place where the garbage and rubbish would be burned up continuously.

❓ *What are the four comparisons Jesus makes that are "better" than hell (v 42-47)?*

Metaphors are used when other words fail to capture the full weight of something—when the reality is so full that one or two ways of talking about it are not enough. Another dominant metaphor for hell in the Bible is being cast into "darkness" (Matthew 8:12). How could hell be a place of darkness if it were aflame for ever?

❓ *What might the symbolism of fire and of darkness communicate about hell?*

These metaphors both point to a total de-struction which stems from being separated from God. In hell, a person does not cease to exist but is cut off from God's presence which gives us all life, light, goodness and joy. This is a far greater suffering than any literal fire or darkness we could imagine.

Salted with fire

In the Old Testament sacrificial system, offerings were not only burnt with fire but also seasoned and purified with salt (Exodus 30:35). Salt represented the commitment that God had made to be faithful to his people, and the commitment the people had therefore made to live according to God's law. Nothing was to be offered without salt (Leviticus 2:13).

In the same way, the followers of Jesus are living burnt offerings purified with salt. The new-covenant community should be marked by the moral purity that comes from committing our lives to God.

❓ *What do you think makes a disciple salty?*

❓ *What difference does the saltiness of disciples make to Christian community (Mark 9:50)?*

A reminder

People tone down the wrath of God because they want to save the idea of the love of God, but the wrath of God is an essential dark backdrop against which we can see the bright, shining beams of the love of God in the gospel of Christ.

⌄ Apply

❓ *How does this passage change or challenge your perception of hell?*

❓ *How can you take seriously the dangers of a proud spirit that disregards "little ones" (v 42) in the faith?*

Bible in a year: 1 Samuel 14 – 16 • Psalm 44

Upside-down kingdom

Jesus is now in a different setting and a different teaching situation. He has left Galilee and travelled south to Judea—to the region around Jerusalem.

Is it lawful?

Read Mark 10:1-12

❓ *Why might the Pharisees want to "test" Jesus, do you think (v 2)?*

There is a hidden landmine behind this question: a heated debate within Jewish culture about how to interpret a phrase in Deuteronomy 24:1 on divorce. One school of thought restricted the meaning to the husband discovering that his wife is committing adultery. The other said that anything could be a reason for divorce— even something as minimal as burning the husband's toast.

❓ *How does Jesus respond (Mark 10:3)?*

The problem with the Pharisees (as usual) is that they are staring at the law and seeing the external issue without stopping to consider the underlying heart issues. The law had to make legal allowance for the people's sinful heart issues. In a perfect world, divorce would not happen, but God gave this commandment because he knew it would.

❓ *How does Jesus eventually lead them to God's heart and his intent for marriage (v 6-9)?*

Divorce will never be understood unless you start by understanding marriage as something God made. Husband and wife are no longer two but one flesh. If God joined them, then man should not separate them.

❓ *How might this view of marriage affect the way Christians treat their spouses?*

Love and correction

Read Mark 10:13-16

❓ *Why do you think Jesus is indignant (v 14)?*

❓ *What have the disciples forgotten (from the previous chapter 9:36-37)?*

❓ *How are Jesus' words in 10:14 similar to 9:39?*

Jesus' indignation is an overflow of love. When you love something and you find it attacked, righteous anger should flare up to protect it. Jesus loves the children by receiving them, and he loves the disciples by correcting them. There is no way that he would wish to be denied the opportunity to take the children in his arms and bless them (10:16).

▼ Apply

❓ *How do these two passages affect your picture of Jesus? Do you tend to see him as either stern and unapproachable or as weakly meek and mild?*

▲ Pray

Give thanks that Jesus loves us as we are, but also loves us too much to keep us that way. Pray for a childlike heart as you listen and learn from his word.

Bible in a year: Psalm 16, Psalm 110 • Joel 2 • Acts 2

Why atheism is foolish

The world around us so often paints Christian belief as foolishness. But in this psalm, David reminds us that the very essence of foolishness is to deny the existence of God.

Read Psalm 14

The fool

The opening words of verse 1 represent the pinnacle of human arrogance and rebellion against God.

> ❓ *What is God's verdict on the atheist in verses 1-3?*

> ❓ *Why does David emphasise the fact that God "looks down" on the situation, do you think (v 2)?*

> ❓ *What does God see when he looks down?*

···· TIME OUT ··

Read Romans 3:9-20

> ❓ *Can you spot where Paul quotes Psalm 14?*

> ❓ *What is the point that Paul is making in this section?*

> ❓ *If we are tempted to feel rather smug in our attitude to the atheist and his folly, what does Paul want us to know?*

The people of God

In verses 4-7, we see how the atheist's unbelief plays itself out in their behaviour. Notice how their animosity towards God is reflected in their mistreatment of God's people.

> ❓ *The people of God do not always have it easy, but what do they have that the evildoers do not have?*

> ❓ *What is it, ultimately, that strikes fear into the heart of the hardened unbeliever (v 5)? What has the unbeliever seen?*

> ❓ *How has the promise of salvation from Zion already been fulfilled in Jesus, and how is it yet to be fulfilled?*

⌄ Apply

> ❓ *Where have you encountered the disdain or even the persecution of unbelievers recently?*

With that in mind, think through...

> ❓ *How does God's verdict on them in v 1-3 help you to think rightly about them?*

> ❓ *How does the reminder of God's presence and protection encourage you not to lose heart?*

> ❓ *How does the hope of v 7 help you to endure opposition?*

⌃ Pray

Thank God that in his kindness he has delivered you from the foolishness of atheism.

Pray for unbelieving friends, that he might open their eyes and give them repentance.

Give thanks for the Lord's protection of his people under pressure.

Praise God that Jesus has come from the heavenly Zion to bring salvation for his people—and that he will come again to complete that salvation.

The rich young man

The disciples have been told to receive the kingdom like a little child. But the rich young man is the polar opposite of childlike.

Read Mark 10:17-22

> ❓ How does the young man's question reveal his beliefs about eternal life (v 17)?
>
> ❓ How does this contrast with what Jesus has just said in verse 15?
>
> ❓ What does the rich young man believe about himself (v 20)?

The problem with the young man's thinking is that the commandments are not a ladder we use to climb up to God by our obedience. They actually function as a mirror to show us that there is no one good except God alone.

···· TIME OUT ·································

Read Exodus 20:2-17

> ❓ What command does Jesus add to his list (Mark 9:18) that is not originally found in the Ten Commandments?

This addition seems to call into question how this man became rich. Could it be that his wealth came from defrauding the poor?

A command

The command Jesus gives (Mark 10:21) reflects the wisdom of another world. The way to become truly rich is to give riches away.

> ❓ What does the young man's reaction show about his true priorities (v 22)?

This is the response of someone trapped in the snare of idolatry. His possessions have taken possession of his heart.

▼ Apply

> ❓ What is the most tempting aspect of money for you? Success? Status? Security?
>
> ❓ How does this passage help you gain a better view of money?

Astonished disciples

Read Mark 10:23-31

The disciples evidently held to the common belief of their time that wealth was a sign of God's blessing or favour.

> ❓ What might Peter be looking for (v 28)?
>
> ❓ What does Jesus remind Peter that they have gained, both in this life and the life to come (v 30)?

We do not boast in what we give up, but in what we gain through what Christ has done for us. When Jesus asks you to deny yourself something, it is always to get something better, longer lasting, and more satisfying. The gospel gives better security than money can give because it gives us our almighty Father.

▲ Pray

Spend some time thanking God for all you have gained because of Jesus' sacrifice.

Third passion prediction

Jesus has stated twice that this journey will end in Jerusalem and that suffering and death await him there. Yet he is the one setting the pace and leading the way.

The disciples cannot fathom why Jesus is so driven to get to Jerusalem. His next piece of teaching should clear up the confusion.

Read Mark 10:32-45

This third prediction is the most detailed. He begins with the title "Son of Man" from Daniel 7:13—who is described as being given "everlasting dominion" (v 14).

> ❷ How will Jesus be rejected by both the Jews and Gentiles (Mark 10:33)?

> ❷ What will he face (v 34)?

···· TIME OUT ···

These details also point back to Isaiah 50 and 53, the songs of the suffering servant.

Read Isaiah 50:5-7

Jesus had set his face "like flint" (50:7) to go to Jerusalem. He had purpose in every step because the plan of the Father was the mission of the Son. The disciples could not see that Daniel's glorious, reigning son of man is also Isaiah's suffering servant.

Ignorant and arrogant

The disciples have been blind to what Jesus has been saying in the last three chapters. But now, James and John finally work up the courage to ask Jesus a question. Could this be the moment when they ask for help with their unbelief? No...

> ❷ What is James and John's underlying desire behind the question (Mark 10:37)?

> ❷ Why do you think the other disciples respond with indignation (v 41)?

> ❷ How is this situation similar to what's just happened in 9:31-34?

> ❷ What is the contrast that Jesus presents (10:42-43)?

Jesus does not rebuke the quest for greatness; he redefines the quest by redefining greatness. True greatness is not about how high you can climb as you step on and over as many people as possible. It is about how low you can go in serving as many people as possible.

⌄ Apply

Without Christ, we are incapable of love in the purest sense because we all have an ulterior motive: we want to gain the love of others. When our love needs are met in the gospel—we, too, can actually love. We can give because we have received.

> ❷ Think about the things you do to serve others. Are there any motives for doing so that aren't so pure? What would a Christlike motivation look like?

⌃ Pray

Praise God for Jesus' love and the freedom we can have from craving the love of others. Ask for help to become satisfied in his love and to serve others out of that gratitude.

Bartimaeus the faithful

In the final section of chapter 10, Mark highlights someone who is a stark contrast with the disciples: Bartimaeus.

Read Mark 10:46-52

This man is disabled and dependent. He is childlike, living on the care of others. But the blind man has eyes to see clearly who Jesus is: the Son of David (v 47), the promised Messiah.

> ❓ *Why might the people have told him to be quiet, do you think (v 48)?*
>
> ❓ *What are the emotions behind Bartimaeus crying out "all the more" (v 48)?*
>
> ❓ *How does Mark describe the way Bartimaeus came to Jesus (v 50)?*

Bartimaeus used his cloak to collect money, like a musician who lays out his guitar case for people to throw in their coins. By faith he now believes he is as good as healed, so he does not need it anymore.

The encounter

Jesus asks a question that stands out as perplexing (v 51). Isn't the answer obvious? This is the same question he asked James and John (v 36). But the answers are totally different. The disciples asked to be seen (v 37), but Bartimaeus asks to see.

> ❓ *How does Bartimaeus act after his healing (v 52)?*

Bartimaeus models what true discipleship is in three ways. First, he sees Jesus rightly. Jesus is the Son of David, who can and will help. Second, he sees himself rightly.

He is totally dependent and in need of help. Third, he responds rightly to Jesus. He leaves all that he has—his cloak—and joyfully follows Jesus on the way.

⌄ Apply

> ❓ *Can you think of some times when you cried for mercy and Jesus answered?*
>
> ❓ *What mercy do you need in your life right now?*
>
> ❓ *How can you follow Bartimaeus' example?*

But now I see

Without Christ, we are all blind. You cannot make yourself see, but you can strategically sit on the path of grace, where you know you will meet Jesus in the preaching of the gospel. Without Christ, we are all spiritual beggars. We have empty hands. But Jesus does not come and give us some spare change; he gives us eternal life at the cost of his own life.

⌃ Pray

A cry for help is the sweetest sound to the Saviour. Do not let fear of what others may think keep you away. Cry out all the more for mercy. See Jesus rightly, see yourself rightly, and respond rightly. Spend some time asking Jesus for what you need.

Jesus in the temple

Mark begins the narration of the last week of Jesus' earthly life. He and his disciples arrive in Jerusalem.

Read Mark 11:1-10

❓ *What kind of reception did Jesus get as he entered Jerusalem (v 8-10)?*

❓ *Who do they think he is (v 10)?*

"Hosanna" means "Oh, save us now!" The people were saying exactly the right thing, but they said more than they knew. They believed that the Messiah would destroy the people oppressing them. They expected Jesus to judge the nations and save them, not to judge them and save the nations.

Read Mark 11:11-21

Jesus' curse is not a case of childish anger. The point of this story is not that Jesus is looking for literal figs. **Read Jeremiah 8:13.**

Jeremiah described the people as being like a fig tree with no figs; they had not grown fruit but rejected what God gave them and were therefore bound for judgment. Jesus is acting out a parable based on this verse.

A fig sandwich

Mark sandwiches Jesus' second trip to the temple with the fig-tree story. We often say that Jesus was driving out those who were misusing the temple to restore it to a house of prayer (Mark 11:17). But in the context of the "bread" of the fig-tree story, I would argue that Jesus was not cleansing the temple but cursing and replacing it, just like he cursed the fig tree that bore no figs.

❓ *What two groups of people did Jesus drive out of the temple (v 15)?*

This was not ordinary commercial activity at all—it was activity which was necessary for the sacrificial systems in place. This was not a mere reform of the temple but a rejection of the whole temple system.

In Jeremiah's day, people were treating the temple like a safe den—a place to go to protect themselves from God's judgment after they had been wicked. They participated in the rituals of the temple, but only because they believed it would keep them safe and allow them to keep sinning. That is what Jeremiah meant in calling God's house a "den of robbers" (Jeremiah 7:11).

❓ *How do people respond to Jesus (Mark 11:18)?*

The people of Jesus' day were also participating in the temple not to pursue God but to hide from judgment and excuse their sinful behaviour.

⌃ Pray

One day the temple worship was going to change, and there would be "a house of prayer for all nations" (Isaiah 56:7). Isaiah 56 promises salvation and blessing for all those typically thought to be excluded from God's people but who "love the name of the Lord" (v 6). With Jesus, that day has arrived. Praise him for his amazing grace that means we can enter into his presence.

Bible in a year: 1 Samuel 24 • Psalm 56, Psalm 120, Psalm 142

Real prayer

Jesus uses this opportune moment to unpack the nature of prayer.

Read Mark 11:22-25

❷ *What does Jesus teach his disciples about what is essential in prayer (v 22, 24)?*

❷ *What is the second thing that Jesus teaches about our hearts in prayer (v 25)?*

The house of prayer

It is important to note that Jesus does not say "a mountain". He says "this mountain" (v 23). He is standing on the Mount of Olives outside Jerusalem, and he can see the Temple Mount and the Dead Sea. He is talking about destroying the temple.

Jesus teaches on prayer here because the temple is to be a house of prayer. If it is replaced, then where can prayer happen? Some people thought that the temple made your prayers more effective. What happens to prayer when the house of prayer is gone?

☑ Apply

It is vital to see that we can have a relationship with God without the formalism and external ritual of the temple.

❷ *How might you rely on rituals or other external things in your relationship with God?*

❷ *How can you see prayer as an act of devotion to God, not just a discipline to master?*

The heart of prayer

C.S. Lewis said, "Everyone thinks forgiveness is a lovely idea until he has something to forgive" (*Mere Christianity*, p 110). Forgiveness is not easy, but failing to forgive reveals a tragic double standard in us. When others fail us, we tend to put the spotlight on their evil actions. When we fail others, we tend to put the spotlight on our good intentions.

···· TIME OUT ··································

Read Matthew 18:21-35

Someone is in spiritual danger if they lose sight of the cross. Unforgiveness happens when someone else's sin becomes bigger than the cross. The debt others owe us seems bigger than the debt we owed God.

❷ *What is the relationship between prayer, faith and a forgiving heart?*

◪ Pray

❷ *Is there someone who you need to forgive today?*

Ask God to reveal if you have been holding onto any unforgiveness in your heart from years gone by. If you are struggling to even want to forgive, ask him to give you a deep understanding of the mercy that you have received—then the help to extend that forgiveness to those who have hurt you.

Bible in a year: 1 Samuel 25 – 26 • Psalm 141, Psalm 54

Rival authorities

Mark introduces Jesus' third trip to the temple.

Read Mark 11:27-33

❷ *What do we already know about the religious leaders' opinion of Jesus and intentions towards him (v 18)?*

❷ *What do you think they are trying to achieve by their question (v 28)?*

The Sanhedrin (or Jewish ruling council) choose a topic on which to tackle Jesus. They want to know what or who gave Jesus the authority to drive out those buying and selling in the temple and teach in radical ways that amazed the crowds. This is a trap—a thinly veiled accusation.

❷ *Who do the leaders think has heaven's authorisation?*

John's baptism

The religious leaders clearly rejected John the Baptist's authority, and so Jesus quizzes them about him.

❷ *Think all the way back to the beginning of Mark's Gospel. How does John's baptism of Jesus answer their question (1:9-11)?*

John was sent with a baptism of repentance for the forgiveness of sins. It did not involve the temple or sacrifices. It was free. By mentioning John, Jesus is once again challenging the Jewish religious system.

❷ *What are the Jewish leaders afraid will happen if they give the popular answer (11:31)?*

❷ *What do they fear will happen if they don't (v 32)?*

❷ *What does their refusal to reply (v 33) show about their true motivation?*

The leaders' hypocrisy is exposed. So Jesus refuses to answer their question—not because he does not know the answer but because he knows their hearts.

Saving face

In the end, what the religious leaders really fear is people, not heaven. All they seem to care about is saving face; they do not see the need to save their souls.

⌄ Apply

❷ *When do you let other people's opinions rather than God's opinion dictate your actions?*

❷ *Are there moments when you are more concerned with proving a point than understanding the truth?*

⌃ Pray

Praise God for the freedom that Jesus' authority brings—the ability to come to him in prayer anytime and in any state.

Confess a recent time you allowed fear of other people to influence your words or decisions and ask Jesus for the wisdom to accept his authority in your life.

Entry requirements

Who will qualify to share eternity with God in heaven? What are God's entry requirements? Questions don't get more significant than this one...

Read Psalm 15

The key question

Every summer, the British royal family hosts a number of garden parties at Buckingham Palace. These are strictly "by invitation only" events—and invitations are hard to come by. Only those who have made outstanding contributions in public service are invited.

David's world is not modern London, of course. It's ancient Jerusalem, the great city built upon Zion's "holy mountain". In his mind's eye is not a palace, but the Lord's dwelling place, his "tent" (the tabernacle, later replaced by the temple). And David's question is this: *who will be invited in?* And more than that, *who will be allowed to live in the Lord's home and in his city?*

Read Hebrews 12:22-24

❷ *Where does the earthly Mount Zion point us?*

❷ *In light of that, what do you think is the answer to the big question that Psalm 15:1 asks?*

The daunting answer

❷ *What is the Lord's answer to David's question (v 2-5)? What kind of person will be admitted?*

❷ *How does this answer make you feel? Where does it leave sinful people like us?*

Read verses 2-5 again, and consider whether there is—or ever has been—anyone who meets God's requirements perfectly.

Hope and challenge

Has someone come to mind?! Only the Lord Jesus has lived perfectly the kind of life required for entry to God's presence. But wonderfully, if we are trusting in him, we are admitted to the heavenly Zion because of his perfect record in righteous living.

That's great news, but it doesn't remove the challenge of these verses, because, if we belong to Jesus, we will be changed by Jesus. His agenda is to make us more like himself. Ultimately, the evidence that we belong to him is that we're growing to be more like him.

⌄ Apply

❷ *Where do verses 2-5 need to challenge the way you live? What will change?*

⌃ Pray

Thank God for Jesus and his perfect record of blameless living—and that we are admitted to heaven because of his merits alone. Thank God for the wonderful prospect of living with him for ever on his "holy mountain".

Ask God to help you to become more like Jesus so that your life reflects his blameless life a little more today than it did yesterday.

A final parable

As a further challenge to the religious leaders, Jesus now tells his final parable in Mark: the story of the tenants of a vineyard.

Read Mark 12:1-12

This is an old story drawn from Isaiah 5, where the vineyard represents God's people. There is a note of surprise in Isaiah about how bad the grapes are in spite of how well God cares for the vineyard. Jesus' parable is even more suspenseful and shocking. The twist in this story is how bad the tenants are—not the vineyard itself but the people who care for it.

❷ *How does the owner of the vineyard display patience (Mark 12:2-5)?*

❷ *The tenants represent the religious leaders (v 12)—so what is Jesus saying about them?*

❷ *How might this parable answer the question posed to Jesus at the end of the last chapter (11:28)?*

Wicked tenants

❷ *What do the tenants want (12:7)?*

❷ *What happens to them (v 9)?*

❷ *Why does the vineyard not end up uninhabited (v 9)?*

Jesus is saying that God will replace the temple system and bring foreigners to become part of his people. The vineyard will belong to the nations after the owner brings judgment on the original tenants.

❷ *How does Jesus show that this very process is what God had planned all along (v 10-11)?*

One of the glories of the temple was the story of the temple architecture. There was a stone that would not fit any part of the building. It was rejected. But in the end, that stone fit perfectly as the cornerstone: the stone that stands at the summit of a corner and holds the whole structure together.

Jesus' parable stressed the rejection and dishonour of the son. Now this prophecy (v 10-11) shows that the rejection of the Son would be reversed and would result in vindication. In the prophecy, the builders are the religious leaders, and the stone that they reject is the Son. After being rejected and discarded, he will become the cornerstone.

✔ Apply

❷ *Does this parable remind you of any circumstances in the world today?*

❷ *How do you respond?*

✔ Pray

Spend some time thanking God for his willingness to send his Son, even in the knowledge that he would be rejected and killed. Praise him that he has made us his people with Jesus as our cornerstone.

Pray for those you know for whom Jesus is a stumbling block—that their eyes would be open to who he is.

A battle of wits

The religious leaders fell victim to the most classic blunder of all time: do not put God to the test.

Read Mark 12:13-17

The first challenge

The Pharisees and the Herodians were two groups of people who could not agree on anything—except that they needed to get rid of Jesus.

> ❓ *How do they try to lure Jesus into a trap (v 14)?*
>
> ❓ *Do they really believe what they're saying?*
>
> ❓ *What two lessons do Jesus' words give us (v 17)?*

We can look at whose likeness is on a coin, but we can also look at any person and ask, "Whose likeness is on this person?" The answer is "God's". Therefore, what should we give back to God? Everything we have! We are accountable to God for what we do with every breath he gives us.

☑ Apply

As we live out the truth of accountability to God, we must recognise that we are not saved by what we give to God, but by what he gives to us: the righteousness of Jesus.

> ❓ *How do you feel about giving your all to him as an act of worship rather than an attempt to be accepted?*

The second challenge

Read Mark 12:18-27

This time the challenge comes from the Sadducees—a group who did not believe in the resurrection of the dead.

> ❓ *How does Jesus frame his response to their question (v 24, 27)?*
>
> ❓ *Why won't anyone be married in the new creation as some are here on earth (v 25)?*
>
> ❓ *How does the present tense of Jesus' quote disprove the Sadducees' position on the resurrection (v 26-27)?*

Marriage between a man and a woman points to the eternal, heavenly marriage between Jesus and his bride, the church—and the symbol can cease when the real thing arrives. God sent his Son into the world to win his bride and defeat death; now the relationship between God and his people is unbreakable.

> ❓ *How should Jesus' words about the resurrection affect the way we live now?*

⌃ Pray

We are not immune to trying the same thing as these groups. We can be quick to wonder if his way really is best. If you're finding life hard, cry out to him about the things you don't understand, believing at the same time that he is wise beyond your imagination.

Bible in a year: 2 Samuel 1 – 3 • Psalm 125

The third challenge

Reading the religious leaders' final challenge is a little bit like watching a tennis match.

Read Mark 12:28-34

There is a back-and-forth between one of the teachers of the law and Jesus, and then we see the conclusion of the match (v 34).

❓ *What does Jesus highlight before he says the first command (v 29)?*

❓ *The man asks for one command, but Jesus gives two. Why can Jesus not separate these commands? (See also 1 John 4:19-21.)*

Remember the context: Jesus has been speaking against what has been happening in the temple. The man has understood that loving God and neighbour mean more than participating in temple activities.

❓ *What do you think the teacher needs to see in order to enter the kingdom (Mark 12:34)?*

⌄ Apply

❓ *What would it look like to take the next steps of obedience in loving God with everything you have and loving others as yourself?*

❓ *What do you need to give to God? Where do you need to step up in love for others?*

Jesus' challenge

Jesus now calls into question the scribes' understanding of the Messiah. Do they really know who they are looking for?

Read Mark 12:35-37

Jesus quotes from Psalm 110:1. He starts with who is saying it—King David (Mark 12:36). The first "Lord" must be a reference to Yahweh. And if Yahweh is "the Lord", then who would a king call "my Lord"? This must be a reference to the Messiah. How can the Messiah be David's son if he is David's Lord (v 37)?

Jesus' question does not deny that the Messiah is the son of David. The Old Testament made it very clear that the Messiah was to be born in David's royal line (2 Samuel 7). Jesus has already been confessed as "the Son of David" by Bartimaeus (Mark 10:47-48). So, the question is not whether the Messiah is the son of David but whether he is *only* the son of David.

❓ *How does the crowd's reaction (v 37) reflect the man's reaction (v 32)?*

It is not enough to say that Jesus is right—we must confess that he is Lord. You can read the Bible or listen to preaching about the identity of Jesus and hear the truth gladly without ever surrendering to it fully. But this truth deserves all or nothing.

⌃ Pray

Ask God to help Jesus' words penetrate your heart as well as your mind. Pray that you would know Jesus as Lord and King over every area of your life.

Rich in faith

Chapter 12 closes with two contrasting pictures: counterfeit devotion to God and true devotion to God.

Read Mark 12:38-44

❓ *What picture does Jesus paint of the teachers of the law in these verses?*

❓ *Why do they do these things?*

❓ *What is the difference between the way the people respond to the religious leaders and the way God responds (v 40)?*

The religious leaders are not just spiritual peacocks that flaunt their devotion for the sake of self-promotion; they are predators. They took advantage of the kindness and hospitality of poor widows and preyed upon it—eating them out of house and home.

It should come as no surprise to see a widow take centre stage in the next story.

The widow's offering

❓ *On the face of it, is Jesus' claim true (v 43)?*

❓ *What is the rationale he uses to support his claim (v 44)?*

The rich are still rich after their apparently generous donations. But the poor woman went from a little to nothing. Her extravagant gift showed that the Lord was her hope and trust and security and treasure—not financial security.

❓ *What do the rich people have in common with the teachers of the law that Jesus has just condemned (v 38-40)?*

There is a contrast in these two passages between the showiness of the religious leaders and the hiddenness of the widow. She gives as an expression of praise, not as a strategy to get praise.

⌄ Apply

❓ *In your life, what would it look like to behave like the religious leaders?*

❓ *What would it look like to behave like the poor widow?*

The widow's trust

My daughter once taught me this lesson in a surprising way. She was going to put money in the offering plate and decided to put in all the money from her little purse. I told her, "Sweetheart, you do not have to put all of it in. You can keep some back for yourself." I will never forget her response: "I don't need money. I have a daddy!"

I found myself greatly rebuked. I want to be rich in faith in the same way. The fact that we have a Father should change the way we think about our need for money.

⌃ Pray

Spend some time meditating on the generosity and goodness of your Father God. Ask him to help you increase your trust in him as you consider how you can give generously to his work.

Bible in a year: 2 Samuel 4 • Psalm 6, Psalm 9, Psalm 17

Signs of the end

Jesus spends so long telling his disciples about what is to come because he wants them to endure to the end and be saved.

Read Mark 13:1-13

The temple's future

❷ *What does the disciple's comment show about what they value (v 1), especially considering Jesus' recent teaching on the temple?*

❷ *Why do you think the disciples' question (v 4) might prompt Jesus to start with a warning (v 5)?*

❷ *What does Jesus tell the disciples to expect (v 6-8)?*

❷ *What is hopeful about the metaphor Jesus uses at the end of verse 8?*

Nothing is worse than pointless pain. But pain that is connected to a purpose is different. Childbirth involves incredible agony, but the joy of holding that newborn baby makes the pain worth it. The strife and pain that Jesus is speaking of are woes that will give birth to a whole new world—better than anything we could imagine.

The disciples' future

❷ *What are the different settings where Jesus says persecution will take place (v 9, 12)?*

❷ *What does Jesus confirm is the reason and purpose of this persecution (v 9)?*

❷ *What is the promise that Jesus gives in the middle of this answer (v 11)?*

❷ *What does Jesus stress is key (v 13)?*

⌄ Apply

Many people want to be certain about the immediate instead of bringing the ultimate into the immediate. Christians have an urgent need to bring "for ever" to bear on what is right now.

❷ *What situations tempt you to forget "for ever"?*

❷ *Who or what encourages you to persevere when the present and future look bleak?*

❷ *Who can you encourage with the truth that there is hope beyond the "now"?*

Stand firm

For every reference to the first coming of Jesus in the Bible, there are eight references to his second coming. Why? Because it is essential for living the life of faith. No matter how hard it is now, we press on through trials because it's worth it.

⌃ Pray

Knowing that Jesus will one day return and set things right is what will also give us the courage and confidence to keep going. Pray that you will be able to see his return above the pain and problems that you face in the here and now. Pray that you will be able to release the need to know what will happen and trust him with the unknowns.

Abomination & tribulation

How should we understand these next verses?

Read Mark 13:14-23

There are three main ways to read this passage:

1. The historical view: Jesus is solely referring to a time soon after his death—AD 70 when the temple in Jerusalem was destroyed.

2. The eschatological view: Jesus is solely referring to the end of the age and his second coming.

3. The third and most common position is to read this passage as a mix of both historical events and imagery of the end times. History consists of repeating cycles and patterns. The destruction of the temple in AD 70 is inextricably linked to the final judgment at the second coming. Some of what Jesus says refers to one event; some refers to the other; some refers to both.

❷ *What do those hearing Jesus' words need to be careful and vigilant about (v 21-22)?*

The 1st-century Jewish historian Josephus used similar language to describe what happened in that time: many messianic imposters arose who tricked the masses. So the historical view would say that Jesus was predicting things that happened in his own time and just afterwards.

But on the eschatological view, these deceivers and false signs will come shortly before the day of the Lord. Jesus' language fits very well with what Paul says about the man of lawlessness (2 Thessalonians 2:9).

Apply

❷ *What do you find encouraging in what Jesus says here?*

❷ *Is there anything you find worrying?*

❷ *Based on the eschatological reading of these verses, what do you think it looks like to "be on your guard" with regard to the second coming?*

Read Mark 13:24-27

❷ *Do you think these verses stretch the historical view too far?*

Read Acts 1:6-11

❷ *What parallels do you see here in Acts?*

The language of gathering God's people comes from Old Testament texts that describe the final gathering (for example Isaiah 45:22). In fact, this passage of Mark is saturated with the language of the prophets and what will happen at the end of the age.

Pray

Ask God to help you make sense of all you have taken in today. Pray that you would be "on your guard", keeping in mind the things to come as well as the day-to-day struggles here and now.

Bible in a year: Psalm 19, Psalm 21 • 1 Chronicles 2 – 3

Satisfaction and security

In a society marked by profound discontent and restlessness, where is true satisfaction to be found?

And in a world rocked by political and financial instability, where is real security to be found?

···· TIME OUT ··

❓ *Where do you think your friends and neighbours look for security and for satisfaction? How about you?*

··

Read Psalm 16

David knew what it was to face disappointment and danger. He was obviously under pressure when he wrote this psalm.

❓ *Where does he find his security and satisfaction?*

❓ *What has David learned about the "other gods" of his unbelieving neighbours (v 4)?*

Israelite families (apart from the priestly families) were given a portion of land as their family inheritance. David was once driven away from his family inheritance by his enemies (1 Samuel 26:19). In Psalm 16:5-6, he says that the Lord himself is his ultimate inheritance.

❓ *What has David learned about the Lord? What benefits do the Lord's people enjoy?*

David had confidence that the Lord would not "abandon [him] to the realm of the dead" nor "let your faithful one see decay".

But David died, so how can we be sure that this promise holds true?

Read Acts 2:23-32

❓ *How do these verses give us assurance that God's promise can be relied upon?*

⌄ Apply

❓ *What "other gods" (Psalm 16:4) are you tempted to run after for satisfaction and security?*

❓ *What steps can you take to keep your "eyes always on the Lord" (v 8) day by day?*

❓ *How can you help yourself and believing friends to be glad and rejoice in the eternal hope set before us (v 9-11)?*

❓ *Why is the hope of the resurrection of the body (v 9-10) so vital for our security and stability in times of danger and uncertainty?*

⌃ Pray

Ask God to deliver you from turning to and living for the gods of this world.

Thank the Lord for his protection of his people and for the wonderful inheritance he has laid up for us.

Praise God for raising Jesus from the dead, and for the certainty that gives us of our future resurrection.

The final warning

This is where it starts to become clear that another timeframe is needed in order to correctly interpret this passage.

Read Mark 13:28-37

Stay awake

If Jesus is talking about the second coming, was Jesus wrong? Because "this generation" (v 30) did not see the second coming.

❓ *What might Jesus be referring to instead, do you think?*

Jesus did something similar back in chapters 8 and 9 when he talked about the Son of Man coming, just before some of them saw him transfigured in power and glory. This gives us a clue as to what is happening here. Jesus is now talking about the events surrounding his death, which are about to take place.

Setting the stage

If the destruction of the temple and the second coming are our only lenses for reading Mark 13, then we miss the way it sets the stage (and the timeframe) for the next section.

❓ *When are the times that the disciples must be awake and not be asleep in case they miss the coming of the Lord (v 35)?*

❓ *Think about Jesus' trial and crucifixion. Do Jesus' words in verse 35 ring any bells? (Hint: see 15:1, 25, 33-34.)*

❓ *Skip forward to the scene in the Garden of Gethsemane in Mark 14:34-41—what*

words are repeated from this passage (13:35-37)?

The way that Mark presents the cross and resurrection of Jesus is so significant. We are not waiting for the end times; we are in the end times. They began with the first coming of Christ. Christ has come. The last days are here. The presence of the future has broken into this present world.

⌄ Apply

❓ *How do you show that you are awake to the reality of the cross and resurrection of Jesus?*

❓ *In what ways do you sometimes find yourself drowsy or sleepy with regard to the reality of Christ's second coming?*

❓ *How can you grow in pursuing the things that are above rather than earthly things?*

---- **TIME OUT** ----------------------------

Read John 2:18-22

Jesus has been talking in Mark about the destruction of the temple. We know from this passage in John that Jesus also spoke of his own body as the temple, saying that it would be destroyed and rebuilt in three days. This is key for our interpretation of the remaining chapters of Mark.

Towards the cross

It is two days before the Passover and Mark does something he does not normally do—he tells us exactly where Jesus is.

Read Mark 14:1-11

No one would expect to see a display of discipleship here, outside Jerusalem, in the house of a leper (perhaps one who Jesus had healed), from this unnamed woman.

❷ *Can you see one of Mark's familiar structural "sandwiches" in this passage? What's at the start and end? What's in the middle?*

Heartfelt worship

Male fellowship among the Jews was not supposed to be broken by women unless they were serving food. Yet Jesus had so captured this woman's heart that she would not be held captive to cultural constraints.

❷ *Considering that women were by and large excluded from the possibility of earning wages, what might the perfume have meant to the woman?*

❷ *What does Jesus' response to her teach us (v 6, 8)?*

Mark presents a glaring contrast in this story between the way the woman values Jesus and the way the disciples value money. In fact, the parallel story in John 12 shows that Judas was the disciple who became indignant with the woman, despite the fact he was a thief (John 12:6). The disciples do not understand that just as this woman broke and poured out her most valuable treasure, so also the Father has sent his greatest treasure in the gift of his Son—whose body will be broken and whose blood will be poured out for the forgiveness of many.

⌃ Pray

This woman's story is now tied to the telling of the gospel story throughout the world (Mark 14:9). Her legacy is her love for Jesus. Do you want that to be the one thing that stands out about your legacy as well?

Spend some time reflecting on how much you value Jesus and ask that you would see him in the same way as this woman.

Preparations

Read Mark 14:12-16

❷ *Why does Mark want to show us the details of how they got the room, do you think (v 13-15)?*

This text heralds the truth that God rules and reigns over this world in minute detail. He is not just generally in control over many things, but meticulously in control of all things.

⌄ Apply

❷ *What do you do with your money? What does that say about your worship?*

❷ *How might this reminder of Jesus' sovereignty help us to be generous like the woman with the perfume?*

Bible in a year: Psalm 85, Psalm 87 – 88, Psalm 93

Betrayal and denial

Mark offers a sandwich once more, continuing the theme of the rejection of Jesus. In the middle, Mark shows the divine purpose behind the drama of betrayal.

Read Mark 14:17-31

Passover commemorated how the Jews were delivered from the Egyptians. The story was retold, remembering the past deliverance and looking forward to the future deliverance that the Messiah would bring.

Two predictions

Jesus predicts his betrayal—it does not take him by surprise; he says it was prophesied (v 21). But he also condemns the person who is to carry out the betrayal.

> ❷ *What does this show us about...*
> • *God's sovereignty?*
> • *our responsibility for our actions?*

Jesus predicts the desertion of the disciples, quoting Zechariah 13:7. God will strike Jesus the shepherd (Mark 14:27). Evil will be used by God to fulfil his saving purpose.

> ❷ *Despite these words, what note of hope does Jesus give (v 28)?*

> ❷ *What does this prophecy trigger in the disciples (v 29, 31)?*

Body and blood

In the middle of it all, Jesus explains the divine design for his death in pictorial form. (v 22-25) He puts his death and resurrection into the symbols offered by the meal. Jesus indicates that his work is really a covenant—a bond in blood that will unite God and his people. Throughout the Old

Testament sacrificial system, the life of a creature was symbolized by its blood. So, Jesus' blood is a reference to his very life.

···· **TIME OUT** ··································

Read Exodus 24:3-8

The blood symbolized the sealing of the covenant. But later prophets announced that a day would come when God would make a new covenant with his people (Jeremiah 31:31-34). Jesus says that day has come. This covenant of grace is about to be purchased and sealed with the lifeblood of the Lamb of God, slain for sinners. This blood will not simply be thrown over the people; they will drink it deeply (figuratively!).

The Last Supper

> ❷ *What does Jesus' choice to continue to eat, speak and sing (Mark 14:22-26) with those who will betray him tell us about his character?*

People who eat and drink have to recognise their need for food and drink. Taking this meal means recognising your need for Jesus' body and blood to save you.

🔼 Pray

Thank Jesus that his death and resurrection brought in this new covenant where your sins are forgiven once and for all. Praise him that he will never let you go.

The agony in Gethsemane

In this next section, Jesus prays three times in the garden, while urging the disciples three times to stay awake.

Keep watch

Read Mark 14:32-41

- ❓ *Why might Jesus have brought Peter, James and John to be close by him (v 33)?*
- ❓ *What does Mark tell us about the severity of Jesus' distress (v 34)?*
- ❓ *What happens to Jesus physically (v 35)?*

We hear the prayer of a heart, soul and will in agony. Jesus is truly God, *and* he is truly human. Here we see Jesus' human will wrestling with the divine will of the Father.

- ❓ *How does Jesus' prayer show both intimacy with and reverence for his Father (v 36)?*

Jesus has taught the disciples to pray, "Your kingdom come, your will be done, on earth as it is in heaven" (Matthew 6:10). He now prays the deepest and truest expression of that prayer ever uttered; he prays in complete submission.

- ❓ *Why does Jesus warn the disciples about their sleeping (Mark 14:38)?*
- ❓ *What can we learn about the nature of prayer from this passage?*

⌄ Apply

If Jesus needed to pray multiple times then we do, too. We naturally shrink back from the prospect of suffering. So persistent prayer is the only way to stay aligned with the Father's will. We don't necessarily need to always pray new things. Sometimes we need to keep praying the same things in order for God's will to be securely fastened within us.

- ❓ *How does this passage show persistent prayer can be for our benefit?*
- ❓ *Is there anything you've given up praying for persistently?*
- ❓ *What requests do you need to bring to God again?*

Asleep again

- ❓ *What is the disciples' reaction to being caught sleeping again (v 40)?*
- ❓ *What might it look like for Jesus' followers to fall asleep instead of keeping watch and praying today?*

A third time, Jesus returns to the disciples after praying alone. Are they still asleep (v 41)? He does not rebuke them—the time to watch and pray is past. Jesus moves forward towards the cross like an arrow aligned with the aim of his Father.

⌃ Pray

Spend some time putting this intimacy in prayer we see from Jesus into practice— bringing your deepest emotions and fears to God. Don't be afraid to ask bold questions. Are you able to pray like Jesus, "not what I will, but what you will"?

The cup of wrath

In the Old Testament, the "cup" of wrath is a symbol of the punishment that God's enemies experience. God now held out the cup of wrath for his Son to drink.

Mark has been helping us to see that, in one sense, Jesus was already being crucified in Gethsemane. His hands and feet were crucified on the cross, but his heart and will were crucified beforehand.

Contemplate this cup for a moment. What would it taste like to drink the cup of God's fiery wrath for every sin (in thought, attitude, or action) that we have ever committed? How much worse would it be to drink the cup of wrath for the sins of many other people?

Betrayed

Read Mark 14:42-52

- ❓ Are the religious leaders actually present (v 43)?
- ❓ The crowd treat Jesus like a robber on the run, but Jesus hasn't been hiding. Why does Jesus tell us they have chosen to seize him now (v 49)?

Read John 18:10-11

This passage reveals the identity of the one "standing near" in Mark 14:47—it's Peter.

- ❓ Does this behaviour fit in line with the profile of Peter that Mark has painted in his account? (Look back at 8:29-33; 14:29-31.)
- ❓ How do Jesus' words in verses 48-49 and John 18:11 show Jesus' readiness to fulfil the will of his Father?

☑ Apply

- ❓ Can you relate to Peter's rash, impulsive decision?
- ❓ What situations might tempt people to flee from Jesus today?
- ❓ How can you make sure you stick closely to Jesus?

Deserted

- ❓ With what attitude does the crowd approach Jesus (Mark 14:43, 46, 48)?
- ❓ How do the disciples treat him once the crowd of armed men have got hold of him (v 50)?
- ❓ Why do you think Mark might tell us about the young man fleeing naked (v 51-52)?

Verses 51-52 can be read as a reference back to Jesus' prediction that people would be in such a hurry to flee that they would not go back to grab their cloak (13:16).

☒ Pray

- ❓ How do you feel as you reflect on the suffering of Jesus in this passage?

Ask God to bring home to you the magnitude of Jesus' sacrifice in these verses. If you are experiencing feelings of betrayal, fear or loneliness today, remember your Saviour can sympathise with you. Thank him that he is beside you in everything you face.

The trial of Jesus

This "trial" is meant to serve justice, but it is actually a mockery of justice.

Read Mark 14:53-65

Notice the way that Mark sets the scene. Jesus and Peter are not far apart. Peter will come back into play soon—but first of all we come to the judicial proceedings against Jesus.

- ❓ *How does Mark emphasise the injustice of the trial (v 55-56)?*
- ❓ *Why do you think Jesus stayed silent (v 61)? (See also Isaiah 53:7.)*
- ❓ *When Jesus speaks, how does he show that he is the true judge (Mark 14:62)?*
- ❓ *What is ironic about the high priest's response (v 63-64)?*

⌄ Apply

The dynamics of this text are still on display today. People look at Jesus and pronounce a judgment over him. Some people even say that when they die, they will have questions to ask God. But this passage reminds us that we should be more concerned about the questions he will have for us.

- ❓ *In what ways can you end up acting as the judge of Jesus instead of recognising that he is your Judge?*

···· TIME OUT ···
Read 1 John 1:7-10

If you are in Christ, then Christ has taken your condemnation. The debt has been paid. The sentence of justice has been served.

- ❓ *Why, in the light of the cross, is it just for God to forgive sinners instead of judge them (v 7)?*
- ❓ *What is the only thing we need to do for forgiveness (v 9)?*

The denial of Peter

While Jesus stands trial before the chief priest, Peter stands on trial before the servant girl of the high priest.

Read Mark 14:66-72

- ❓ *Considering this passage, do you see the irony again in what has been shouted at Jesus (v 65)?*
- ❓ *To what lengths does Peter go to deny Jesus (v 71)?*
- ❓ *What might Peter have realised about himself when he remembers Jesus' words (v 72)?*

Both Peter and the chief priests have not understood the truth of who Jesus is—but Jesus is crystal clear that he is the prophesied Messiah (v 62). See Daniel 7:13-14.

⌃ Pray

Have you ever found yourself ashamed of the way you've represented (or misrepresented) Jesus? Bring that shame to him now, knowing that our guilt is the very reason he went through this trial, and that he wants to redeem and restore you, just as he did with Peter.

The believer's reward

We can easily feel surprised when those who don't know Jesus seem to have an easier and happier time of it than we do.

But David reminds us of where our true reward is found.

Read Psalm 17

David is under attack from wicked people who want to do him harm. This psalm is a prayer (see the psalm's heading), asking God for rescue and protection.

Two foundations

David begins his prayer by declaring his integrity to God. His personal integrity is his basis for asking God for protection and vindication (v 1-5).

We quickly encounter a big speed bump (possibly even a brick wall!) when we try to echo David's prayer for ourselves. Not many of us can say that we have "planned no evil", that we have "not transgressed" in what we have said (v 3), and that our "steps have held to your paths" (v 5) consistently.

The 6th-century bishop Augustine once said that Jesus is the choirmaster who leads his people in singing the psalms. He sings them first—they are true of him, the true Davidic King—and we sing them "in him", as people saved by him and united to him by the work of his Spirit.

> ❓ *In light of that insight, how can you and I possibly echo the prayer of verses 1-5, expecting the Lord to answer us? Whose integrity is the basis of our plea?*

> ❓ *What does David use as the basis of his request in v 6-9? Why is he confident that God will answer and help him?*

> ❓ *How have we seen God's "great love" expressed to us and for us? (Hint: read John 3:16.)*

> ❓ *How can we know that we are the beloved "apple of [his] eye"? (Hint: read 1 John 3:1.)*

> ❓ *How is all this a comfort and encouragement in times of opposition and attack?*

Two outlooks on life

> ❓ *What is the difference between David's outlook and the outlook of the wicked people (Psalm 17:10-15)?*

> ❓ *What is the ultimate hope and delight of the believer? Why is this prospect so good?*

🔼 Pray

Ask God to help you to so delight in the prospect of seeing him face to face that the rewards of this present life will loosen their grip on your heart today.

If you are facing opposition from unbelievers, ask the Lord to help you to draw comfort and steadfastness from the sure hope of seeing him.

The divine King

Chapter 14 showed Jesus being forsaken by the Jews. Chapter 15 now highlights how Jesus is forsaken by the Gentiles.

Read Mark 15:1-15

Will Mark's readers reject Jesus, too, like everyone in the narrative? Or do we have eyes to see and believe what is happening beneath the surface?

Jesus and Pilate

❓ *What does Pilate understand about Jesus' arrest (v 10)?*

❓ *Why might Pilate be amazed at Jesus' silence (v 5)?*

❓ *What do Pilate's questions to the crowd reveal about his feelings towards Jesus (v 9, 12, 14)?*

❓ *What influences Pilate's actions in the end (v 15)?*

Deep injustice

❓ *Why might Barabbas be preferable to Jesus as a Messiah figure for the crowd (v 7)?*

❓ *How is Barabbas's freedom a picture of our own freedom in Christ (v 15)?*

❓ *Can you picture how Barabbas might have reacted to this news?*

When he saw Jesus getting condemned, scourged, mocked, beaten, and murdered, do you think Barabbas ever thought, *that should be me and should not be him?*

 ## Apply

Guilt and shame are real. Sins and failures lead to inner wounds. People can feel so weighed down that they feel the need to punish themselves. But it is in the shedding of Jesus' blood that there is healing.

❓ *Do you ever feel so weighed down with shame that you feel the need to punish yourself, in either small ways or destructive, harmful ways?*

❓ *How does this reminder of Jesus' undeserved sentence and Barabbas's un-earned freedom help you to see that you are freed from the need for punishment?*

Jesus and the soldiers

Read Mark 15:16-20

The irony is unmistakable. The purple robe, the crown of thorns, the chanting and acclaiming as "King of the Jews", the staff, the kneeling and bowing—it all bears royal connotations. They are clearly mocking him, but just as clearly, we can recognise the truth hidden behind the scorn.

Pray

Seeing the truth of Jesus' divinity means that you can no longer live as the king of your life or try to save yourself. In your time of prayer, embrace him as Saviour, hail him as Lord and worship him as God.

The cross of Christ

There's a danger that the cross can become to us like a painting that we hang on our walls. We believe it, but if we are honest, it has simply blended into the background.

Read Mark 15:21-39

Reality of the cross

Mark calls attention to many background details that he does not want us to miss. He wants to understand that these events are incredibly painful but completely purposeful. God's prophesied plan is unfolding but the people witnessing this event do not have eyes to see it. Do we?

❤ Apply

- ❓ *Are you ever discouraged by all the ways that people mock, slander, and slight the worth of Jesus today?*
- ❓ *In the midst of that mockery, what hope does this passage give you personally?*
- ❓ *What comfort does Mark's account of the lead-up to the cross give us in times when we ourselves are suffering?*

Rejection

- ❓ *How does Mark show the blindness of those passing by (v 29)?*
- ❓ *What irony can be found in the words of the chief priests and teachers of the law (v 31-32)?*
- ❓ *Considering the pain and suffocation of the cross, what does that say to you about the actions of those who were crucified alongside him (v 32)?*

- ❓ *What might the darkness in the afternoon represent (v 33)?*
- ❓ *What is the final and deepest rejection that Jesus experiences (v 34)?*

The Father, who has eyes too pure to behold sin, turns his face away from his Son for the first and only time. Jesus endures a moment of separation from God. This is far worse than the mocking, scourging and crucifixion. This is the searing pain of the separation and damnation of God.

Response to the cross

- ❓ *Why might the Roman centurion have been an unlikely person to see the cross of Jesus as the victory of God's Son (v 39)?*
- ❓ *How does his response provide an answer to Jesus' question (v 34)?*

The cross is the one safe place for sinners to run to. Here we have the answer to the cry of Jesus, "Why have you forsaken me?" The answer is: so that we would never be forsaken.

❤ Pray

Do you ever find that you have become numb to the glories of the cross because the story is so familiar? Read the passage slowly again—ask your Father to help you experience the story afresh and respond in thanksgiving.

The women at a distance

It is now Friday evening, and there is a rush to bury Jesus before the Sabbath day starts.

Read Mark 15:40-47

Mary is Jesus' mother (see Mark 6:3). Salome is probably the wife of Zebedee and the mother of James and John (see Matthew 27:56). Mary Magdalene and Salome were Jesus' friends. His mother, Mary, was his nearest kin. They used to follow him and minister to him in Galilee (Mark 15:41). Why is it significant that they are looking "from a distance" (v 40)? This is an allusion to Psalm 38:11: "My friends and companions avoid me because of my wounds; my neighbours stay far away". Now, in Jerusalem, they look at him from a distance as he is considered a plague—condemned and cursed.

A disciple's request

❷ *Who is described as taking an active role in the burial of Jesus (Mark 15:43)?*

❷ *Is his position surprising?*

❷ *What does it take to approach Pilate with this request (v 43)?*

Roman law made it clear that the penalty for capital crimes included the loss of all honour in death—even burial. Part of the shame of crucifixion was to show that no one cared for you. You were left to rot on the cross or be eaten by animals or birds. It would require courage even for a family member to ask for the body of someone convicted of high treason.

❷ *Why might Pilate have granted this unusual request (v 45)?*

A surprising burial

A tomb cut out of rock (v 46) would have been very expensive. In fact, the detail of a stone being rolled against the entrance fits the picture of a very fine tomb indeed for this time period.

Jesus died as a convicted criminal but was buried like a rich man. This matters because it was a fulfilment of Isaiah 53:9: "He was assigned a grave with the wicked, and with the rich in his death, though he had done no violence, nor was any deceit in his mouth".

❷ *What does the detail and timing of everything unfolding in this story tell us?*

❷ *Why is it so important that the story of the cross has so many links with the Old Testament?*

Mary Magdalene and Mary the mother of Jesus saw where Joseph had laid Jesus (Mark 15:47). This is a signal to us that the women got the identity of the tomb right—that is, they went to the right tomb on Sunday morning.

⌃ Pray

The day before his resurrection, Jesus' followers were left bereft and confused. If you're experiencing similar emotions and feel like you can't see or feel God's presence, praise him that Jesus is alive and will one day return to us in glory.

The women at the tomb

Jesus died on Passover (Friday) and rested in the grave on the Sabbath (Saturday). What would happen on the first day of the week (Sunday)?

Read Mark 16:1-8

Attempted anointing

❷ *What does the time of day (v 2) and the women's intention (v 1) show about their dedication to Jesus?*

❷ *But does anyone seem to have believed Jesus' claim that he would rise on the third day?*

All the women's preparations to deal with death have left them unprepared to deal with resurrected life!

❷ *Why might the angel have mentioned Peter specifically by name (v 7)?*

The word of the angel is a message of hope, not scorn, for Peter and the disciples.

The women's testimony

Jewish culture did not place any value on the testimony of women—it was not even admissible in court.

❷ *Does the fact that the women were the first witnesses to the resurrection fit any themes we have seen throughout Mark?*

❷ *Why does this detail show the validity of this Gospel account?*

···· TIME OUT ·······································

Read Mark 16:9-20

I do not think Mark wrote verses 9-20, but that others added it later, for these reasons:

- It is not found in our oldest, most reliable Greek New Testament manuscripts.
- It is not mentioned in the writings of early Christians.
- The language is different from the rest of Mark, introducing many new words.
- The style of writing is different. "Lord Jesus" (v 19) is a phrase which seems to come from later Christian worship.
- It does not flow well. Mary Magdalene is introduced as if for the first time (v 9).

A surprising ending

Re-read Mark 16:8

Every time Jesus does something to demonstrate his deity in Mark's Gospel, the response of the people is the same: fear. Mark is closing his account by saying, *The gospel of Jesus Christ, the Son of God, is an event that shatters all our categories and leaves us with shock and awe. It is both awesome and terrifying.*

⌃ Pray

Ask God to help you put all your hope in the one hope that can't fail or die—because he has already defeated death.

⌄ Apply

❷ *How is God calling you to respond to Mark's Gospel?*

❷ *What do you most want to remember?*

1 THESSALONIANS: In brief

As Paul begins his first letter to the church in Thessalonica, he explains in a brief set of words who these believers really are—and who we are today.

Read 1 Thessalonians 1:1

These believers are "in" Thessalonica, but they're also "in" God the Father and the Lord Jesus Christ. They're united with God, connected to him, under his protection.

They're also recipients of grace and peace. This isn't just a throwaway greeting—these are glorious, big words! Grace means saving favour that we did not deserve. In fact, we deserved the opposite. Yet God saved us. A Christian is defined by this grace, and the peace that comes along with it.

⌃ Pray

Pause to reflect on this for a moment. Consider what it means to you to be defined by being in Christ, full of grace and peace. How does this change you? How could it affect your day? What do you want to say to God about this?

Grace-formed lives

Next Paul gives thanks to God for his work in the Thessalonian Christians' lives.

Read 1 Thessalonians 1:2-6

> ❓ *In verse 3, how do the Thessalonians live, and how is this evidence of God being at work in them?*

> ❓ *In verses 4-5, how did God's work among these believers begin?*

⌄ Apply

> ❓ *Where do you see God at work in your own life? In what ways do you show faith that works, love that labours, and hope that stands firm?*

> ❓ *In what ways do you long for God to work in you more?*

Paul wants us to know here that God's love is unconditional. He does not love us because of what we do. He chose us before the creation of the world, and then worked in us to produce faith, love and hope. If you look at your life and doubt that God could be pleased with you, know that if you are a believer, you are truly, unconditionally loved.

The Spirit's work

Paul says that the message of the gospel came to the Thessalonian believers with power (v 5). As they listened to the truth about Jesus, the Holy Spirit opened their hearts and they became convinced. But not just that: they felt joy. Their priorities changed so quickly that, even in the midst of affliction, they were joyful.

⌃ Pray

Invite the Holy Spirit to continue to be at work in your life. Praise God for others you know whose lives show evidence of his grace, and pray for those who need confidence and joy in God's love for them.

Reports ring out

Paul has been giving thanks to God for his work in the Thessalonian believers' lives—and he still has more to say.

Read 1 Thessalonians 1:6-10

❓ *Who was impacted when the Thessalonians heard Paul's gospel message and became Christians?*

❓ *What is being reported about them?*

This was a church whose reputation preceded them—and it was a godly reputation. Paul would start to tell people about this church, and the people would say, "We've already heard about them!" If we want our churches to enjoy a similar reputation, we need to learn three things that Paul explores in these verses.

1. The gospel, visible

These believers' conversion was dramatic. Their lives changed. And so the power of the Spirit was manifested to the watching world. The gospel was made visible.

❓ *Who did the believers become like?*

❓ *What do you think this might have looked like?*

2. Conversion defined

Turning and serving—that's how Paul describes conversion in verse 9. The Thessalonians were worshipping idols, but now they worship God.

❓ *How is that different to simply changing what you believe?*

❓ *An idol is anything in which we seek*

security or satisfaction instead of in God. What could it look like in someone's life today to turn from idols and serve God instead?

3. Life looking forward

Verse 10 makes it clear that the new believers are now confidently awaiting Jesus' return.

❓ *Why are they looking forward to this?*

❓ *How would this change their lives?*

☑ Apply

A friend of mine once had a conversation with the pastor of a church in a small town in the south of the US where they had had 200 baptisms in one year. My friend said, "You must have set your town on its ear!" The pastor replied, "What do you mean?" And my friend said, "You're telling me that 200 people have been converted to the Lord in a town of 5,000, and not everybody is talking about it?"

❓ *Real conversion produces real change. Do outsiders notice that the gospel has made a difference in your church community? And in your life?*

Take some time to pray for the witness of your church to the people around you. As you do, give thanks that the Holy Spirit works change in us—it's not something we do on our own.

Victory—his and ours

This psalm recounts a great victory and deliverance for the Lord's king. But how is this anything more than just an encouraging history lesson for us?

Read Psalm 18

In our house, we have a silver napkin ring with an engraving saying it was given to someone we have never met, by someone we have never met, in the year 1915, a long time before any of us were born. It feels as though it is not ours; it was not bought or engraved for us, and its purchase predated the birth of all our living relatives. And yet it is ours—because it was given to a relative of a previous generation and was handed down to us.

Psalm 18 speaks of a victory that was first given to David, God's king, thousands of years ago (have a look at the psalm's heading). At first sight it looks as though you and I could never join in the words of this psalm and speak them as our own. But the fruit of the victory spoken of here is handed down to God's people of every age. We share in it. And so we really can learn to sing and pray the words of this psalm as our own.

Look again at verse 50, which is the key to understanding this. The "anointed" is another way of saying the "Messiah" or "Christ". So yes, God saved David from Saul, and the psalm recounts that great salvation. But in an even greater and ultimate display of power, God saved Jesus, the anointed one, from his enemies and from the grave. And if we belong to Jesus, we are the "Anointed" King's descendants.

So, read through the psalm again, and ask these questions:

- ❷ *How and when did God give King Jesus the victory described here?*
- ❷ *Where does the victory of Jesus shine through particularly clearly in these verses?*
- ❷ *Why is Jesus' victory over the grave a victory for us too?*

Here in the psalm David models how we ought to respond to the Lord's salvation (see especially v 1, 46-50).

- ❷ *What is the right response to God's salvation?*

☖ Pray

Spend a few minutes simply praising and thanking the Lord for his great salvation in Jesus.

The purest motives

It seems that there are people in Thessalonica who are trying to undermine Paul's credibility—painting what he did there in a bad light.

In 1 Thessalonians 2 Paul defends the way he acted when he was among the Thessalonians. As he does so, he provides us with principles for how ministry is to be done and why.

Pray

Think about your ministry for a moment. This can be any way in which you minister to others, either practically or with words. Consider how you serve and why. Ask God to refine your heart and make your service more fruitful through today's study.

You know how it was

Read 1 Thessalonians 2:1-7a

❓ *Let's imagine what people in Thessalonica were saying about Paul. How does what Paul says respond to the following accusations?*
  - *His ministry was pointless.*
  - *He was a coward.*
  - *He was only there for what he himself could get out of it.*

Paul is an example to us. To him, the message Jesus has entrusted to him is the most important thing in his life. He takes his mission seriously—not only because it comes from God but because he can please God by it (v 4).

❓ *What did this motivation cause Paul to do (v 2), and not to do (v 5-6)?*

Apply

❓ *In what situations are you tempted to please people and not God?*

❓ *What does that lead you to do or not do?*

❓ *How could it help you to see yourself as someone who has been entrusted with God's message?*

Like young children

Paul's position as an apostle—someone specifically commissioned by the risen Lord Jesus—was a special one. But he never abused it. He sought to make himself low so that no one could accuse him of self-promotion. This is an immense challenge to us today! It's so easy to think we have all the answers and to want others to admire or reward us for our service. But Paul calls us to have the same mindset as Christ: one of lowliness, humility and self-sacrifice (Philippians 2:6-8).

Apply

Sometimes we do need to assert our authority (for example when working with children). But even then, we can still have a servant-hearted mindset.

❓ *What would it look like for those who are in a position of leadership to have the humility of Paul and of Jesus?*

A mother and a father

How do you behave towards your fellow believers?

We can sometimes think of Paul as a hard, uncompromising man. But that's not the picture we see in these next verses. No, he describes himself and his companions as being full of gentleness, affection and love.

Read 1 Thessalonians 2:7-12

Total commitment

The image of a "nursing mother" is very specific. This is a mother who is breastfeeding a small baby. She feeds him every few hours. She gets up in the middle of the night to comfort him. She cuddles and plays with him. It's an image of 24-hour commitment.

> ❓ *How does Paul express his own commitment to the believers (v 8)?*

> ❓ *What did this lead him to do (v 9)?*

Paul and his companions worked to support themselves financially so that the fledgling Christians in Thessalonica did not have to support them. Paul had a right to be paid (see 1 Corinthians 9:11, 14), but he did not want to be a burden to the Thessalonians.

Constant comfort

> ❓ *What kind of "father" was Paul to the new believers (1 Thessalonians 2:10-12)?*

Paul says his conduct was blameless. This doesn't mean he was without sin. Of course he sinned; all of us do. But he knows that in these matters, he was living as God would have him live. His behaviour was above reproach—no one could reasonably accuse him of wrongdoing. And this was not for Paul's own sake; it was for the sake of his children in the faith.

> ❓ *What was Paul's aim—what did he urge the believers to do (v 12)?*

> ❓ *Why was Paul's own behaviour and lifestyle important, then?*

⌄ Apply

How do you behave towards your fellow believers? Are you gentle, committed, above reproach? Do you encourage and comfort those around you? What do you think is the impact of your life on others? Ask God to give you insight into your own behaviour.

A life worthy of God

Fortunately for us, living Christianly is not just a matter of trying our hardest to be like Paul. We can't manage that in our own strength! But two words that Paul uses at the end of verse 12 hint at how we can begin to walk in a manner worthy of God. What motivates us, and what empowers us? It's all about God's kingdom and God's glory.

⌃ Pray

Spend some time thanking God for calling you into his kingdom. Ask for his help to live for his glory in every interaction.

Bible in a year: 2 Samuel 16 – 17 • Psalm 4, Psalm 12

The word at work

If someone asked you what the Bible is, what would you say?

Read 1 Thessalonians 2:13

❷ *What did the new believers in Thessalonica understand about Paul's message?*

❷ *What does the word of God do?*

Paul is describing the gospel message he brought to Thessalonica. But this also applies to the Bible, and to the preaching of the Bible. We need to understand that God is at work in us through his word. Every time a church gathers under God's word, the congregation is there to experience an encounter between their souls and the living God!

⌃ Pray

What does your attitude tend to be as you approach God's word—either alone or as someone preaches? Take a moment to reflect and marvel at how God works through his word. Ask for his help in having a godly and reverent attitude towards it.

Faithful in suffering

Read 1 Thessalonians 2:14-16

Paul now commends the Thessalonians for becoming imitators of the churches in Judea. Specifically, they are imitators in the sense of continuing to believe in and trust the Lord even while they're experiencing persecution. These Christians are willing to suffer for Christ.

Both the Jewish Christians in Judea and the Greek Christians in Thessalonica have suffered opposition from their own countrymen.

❷ *What does this opposition look like (v 15-16)?*

···· **TIME OUT** ····································

Very sadly, this passage has sometimes been interpreted as anti-Semitic. But Paul did not hate Jews; he was himself Jewish. In Romans 9:3 he speaks passionately of his wish that his fellow Jews would put their faith in Jesus. What Paul is denouncing in 1 Thessalonians 2 is the unbelief and sin of certain Jews—and of many non-Jews (v 14).

··

The whole world stands condemned by God and is under his just judgment because of sin—if they do not trust in Christ. Yet there is hope for us all, Jew and non-Jew, if we honour Christ as Lord.

⌃ Pray

Can you think of someone who experiences affliction because of Christ—whether persecution for their beliefs, or suffering because they deny themselves to serve others? Pause and give thanks for them.

Then think of those you know who have rejected Christ. Pray that God will have mercy and that they will turn to trust in him as their Lord.

Our glory and joy

What do you find it easiest to be grateful for?

We may often think of the earthly blessings God gives us: food, clothes, resources. But what about gratitude for other people? Do we find ourselves being blessed when we see God's word at work in somebody else's life—even if that doesn't directly impact us?

Read 1 Thessalonians 2:13, 17-20

❓ *How does the Thessalonian Christians' faith affect Paul?*

❓ *How would you describe his feelings and attitude towards them?*

Blocked

Paul has been desperate to visit the Thessalonians, but has been unable to.

What does he mean by "Satan blocked our way"? Some commentators think that there was opposition to his ministry in Thessalonica—perhaps the civil leaders had banned him from returning. Another reason could be the sin and scandals he was dealing with in other churches. A third interpretation is that Paul's "thorn in the flesh" (a mysterious ailment or weakness mentioned in 2 Corinthians 12:7) prevented him from going. Whichever it is, Paul is clear that Satan was behind his inability to get back to the Thessalonians.

This has huge implications. There is a real evil being in this world who wants to test us and destroy us. We need to factor that in to our thinking—not so that we absolve ourselves of any personal responsibility ("the devil made me do it") but so that we seek the Lord Jesus Christ, who is stronger than the devil. Satan works to hinder, accuse, and tempt us, but Jesus is victorious.

A pastor's glory

What enables Paul to bear the persecution and pressure? The Thessalonians themselves. They are Paul's joy and crown—the thing he boasts about. Paul knows that one day he will see these believers safe home with the Lord Jesus. That's the reward he's looking forward to.

This is what it looks like to live in light of Jesus' return. It's not only about ourselves—who we worship and how we behave. It's also about giving ourselves to helping others—praying for, teaching, supporting, encouraging, and rebuking our fellow believers, filled with the joyful hope that one day we will see them before Jesus, being welcomed home.

Pray

Pray for your brothers and sisters in the faith. Spend as much time as you can praising God for his work in them. Then pray that God will continue to strengthen them and uphold their faith.

Sending Timothy

What's the goal of ministry? Paul reveals one answer to that question in today's passage.

Read 1 Thessalonians 3:1-8

❓ *What has been happening to Paul (v 4)?*

❓ *How did he fear the Thessalonians would respond to the news (v 3, 5)?*

Suffering and trials should not be a surprise to Christians. We are "destined" for them—they are certain to come. But we can be prepared to endure afflictions by being established and strengthened in our faith.

❓ *How did Paul seek to strengthen the Thessalonians' faith (v 2)?*

❓ *What do you think Timothy might have said to the believers in Thessalonica?*

☑ Apply

❓ *How strong do you feel in your faith at the moment?*

❓ *What would it look like for you to be more firmly established in your knowledge of God?*

❓ *What would it look like for you to be more encouraged and confident in your trust of God?*

❓ *What is one thing you could do over the coming weeks to help you grow and be strengthened?*

Faith and love

❓ *What good news does Timothy bring back from Thessalonica (v 6)?*

❓ *How does Paul respond to this (v 7-8)?*

In verse 6, the phrase "good news" is a specific word that Paul usually uses to refer to the gospel message. So he is saying, *Timothy brought me gospel.* That's how wonderful the news of the Thessalonians' faith is!

Paul's priorities here should challenge us. What do we dream of for our lives, and for our children's lives? To marry a nice person, have a good job, be financially secure, achieve great things? Far more important than any of those is standing firm in Christ and growing in faith and love. That's what we should be praying, above all, for our loved ones.

John Calvin wrote that these two words, faith and love, are "the entire sum of true piety". That is, all godliness can be summed up in faith and love.

⌃ Pray

Pray for yourself. Ask God to grow you in faith and love, and to prepare you well to stand firm when times are hard.

Pray for those you serve at church or elsewhere. Ask God to show you who you could encourage or strengthen in their faith.

Pray for your family members and closest friends. Ask God to cause them to stand firm in Christ and to grow in faith and love.

When love overflows

Truth or love—which is more important to you instinctively?

In today's passage we see how truth and love are supposed to work *together*.

What is lacking

Read 1 Thessalonians 3:9-11

What does Paul mean by "supply what is lacking"? Faith comes from God—Paul can't create it or grow it. What he means to do is to teach the Thessalonians the word of God. They have the basics, but they need to know more so that their faith can grow. As he puts it in Romans 10:17, "Faith comes from hearing, and hearing through the word of Christ" (ESV).

The Thessalonians need to know more truth, and Paul longs to teach it to them. But what is the point of that?

Love increases

Read 1 Thessalonians 3:12-13

❓ *What does Paul pray for the Thessalonians in these verses?*

I often say to my seminary students, "You can learn as much theology as you want, and still go home and be a jerk to your wife". It's very possible to miss the point of how truth functions. God's truth is supposed to change the way we act.

❓ *Can you think of an example of this in your own life? As you look back, how have you changed since you became a*

Christian? And how has your knowledge about God grown? Can you see how the two are related?

Blameless and holy

If the result of being grounded in God's word is to grow in love, the result of growing in love is to be established in holiness.

❓ *How does this work? Why does loving others and relating to others make us more godly? Why might it be hard to grow in holiness if we spent all our time alone?*

Let's say that I decide that I'm going to be a more faithful person. I can't do that by myself. There has to be someone around to be faithful to. Even with more "solo" virtues like joy or peace, it's when someone else is making life difficult that we really grow and become more established in godliness.

Other people can also keep us accountable—rebuking us when they spot our sin or encouraging us when they see positive growth. When we love each other and seek to help each other grow in love, that's when we increase and abound in love as a community.

⌃ Pray

Use the words of Paul's prayer to help you pray for your own church community.

He is not silent

It is a popular misconception that God is more or less silent and that it's our job to find out about him as best we can. Psalm 19 explodes that myth for us.

Read Psalm 19

The word displayed

After a nine-and-a-half-year journey, in 2015 the US probe New Horizons finally reached Pluto and began sending back the first detailed pictures we'd ever seen of that planet. The images were wonderful and fascinating. It's a whole other world—a world complete with mountains and valleys and colour and contour. And it's just one little dot in the vast and magnificent starry heavens that declare God's glory. The pictures that came back from the probe should move us to praise the Creator for the wonders of his creation.

❷ *How has God spoken, according to verses 1-6?*

❷ *What does this "word" say about him?*

❷ *How far does this word travel (v 4)? Why does that matter?*

···· **TIME OUT** ·····································

Read Romans 1:18-20

❷ *What are some of the implications of the fact that God has made himself known in this way?*

The word written

In Psalm 19:7 David switches from using the more universal name of "God" to the more personal name of "LORD"—a name that highlights his covenant relationship with his chosen people, Israel. This change reminds us that God's revelation in creation will tell us of his existence, but only his written word in Scripture can lead us to a saving, personal and covenantal relationship with him.

❷ *What is the Lord's word like, and what can it do? What are the benefits for us of reading and knowing his word?*

❷ *If you struggle to find motivation to read his word, which of these truths have you forgotten or stopped believing?*

We have seen what the word does in verses 7-11, and in verses 12-13 we see something of the effect of the word on the psalmist's heart. He sees that he needs to respond to God's word personally. And the same is true for us.

⌃ Pray

Examine your heart in light of verses 12-14, and echo the psalmist's prayer in your own words. Then praise God for how he has revealed himself through his creation, and his word, and his Son, through whom all things were made and about whom all Scripture speaks.

Live to please God

So far in 1 Thessalonians, Paul has been speaking about his readers' faith and reminding them of his past ministry among them. Now it's time for instructions.

Read 1 Thessalonians 4:1-8

❓ *What is Paul's headline instruction in verse 1?*

❓ *What motivation to obey does Paul give the believers (v 2, 3, 8)?*

Pleasing and personal

The apostle Paul is like a personal trainer, pushing Christians in order to help them to achieve their goal. He is not simply telling them off or giving them a list of dry instructions. He is urging them on to be more like their Saviour.

He is also inviting them to please God through the way they live. It isn't that God is hard to please. No, Paul's instructions are an encouragement to please someone who is already disposed to be pleased—like a kind father. The Thessalonians can view their obedience to God in light of the pleasure the Lord takes in them.

🔼 Pray

Pause to reflect on this before we look at Paul's more specific instructions. Talk to God as a kind Father who wants to be pleased. Ask for his help in pushing on into greater godliness.

Sexually pure

There is a clear biblical pattern for sexual morality: sex is designed to be within a committed and faithful lifelong marriage between one man and one woman. Yet it is all too easy for Christians to be tempted into immorality—whether it's watching pornography, acting upon same-sex attraction, or having sex outside of marriage.

❓ *What is a sexually immoral person not managing to do (v 4)?*

❓ *Why do you think this is a bad thing for them personally?*

❓ *How does it impact others (v 5)?*

❓ *How does it affect the person's relationship with God (v 6)?*

Why do Christians care about sexual purity? It's not because we are repressed or prudish. It's because we love God and we love people. We care about living distinctive lives that put the gospel on display. We care about honouring the God who dwells in us by his Spirit. We care about treating others with respect and love.

🔽 Apply

If you have given in to the temptation to live in sexual immorality of any kind, you need to repent of those sins—and remember that the blood of Christ is sufficient to cover them.

Ask for the Spirit's help, since it's God's will to make you holy (v 3, 8). Pray this for yourself even if you have not fallen into sexual sin.

Mind your own business

*Did you ever realise **that** phrase was in the Bible?!*

But Paul's "mind your own business" may not be quite the same as ours.

Read 1 Thessalonians 4:9-12

Brotherly love

Paul compliments the believers on the good job they're doing of showing love—not only to each other but also to visiting believers from other cities.

> ❷ *How did they learn to love like this (v 9)?*
>
> ❷ *How do you think the Thessalonians would have felt to hear that truth, and why?*

···· TIME OUT ·······································

Scholars think that the phrase "taught by God" (which is actually one word in Greek) is a reference to Isaiah 54:13, where God promised that there would be a day when he himself would teach his children. It's a promise about the new covenant, when God's laws would be directly written on his people's hearts (see Jeremiah 31:33). Jesus brought about the new covenant—so the love shown by the Thessalonians is proof of the fulfilment of that Old Testament promise.

▾ Apply

The Thessalonians love each other—but Paul urges them to do so more and more.

> ❷ *Consider how you love those around you. Do you see your fellow church members as being like your brothers and sisters— your blood kin? What are you doing to contribute to that family? How are you loving other brothers and sisters outside your local church?*

Spend some time in prayer asking God to make you more and more loving.

Godly work

> ❷ *What kind of daily life does Paul call his readers to live, and why (1 Thessalonians 4:11-12)?*

"Lead a quiet life" means avoiding public controversy. They're not to gather crowds around them but just to get on with living faithfully. "Mind your own business" means not being busybodies. They're to care for each other, but not to meddle. "Work with your hands" means working hard to support themselves, if they are able, so as to avoid being a burden on others. (It isn't that manual labour is more godly than office work!)

▴ Pray

Take time to think through those three instructions for yourself. Ask God to show you where you could please him by your obedience to these commands. Ask him to work in your life so that you win the respect of non-believers—not for your own sake, but for the Lord's.

Bible in a year: 1 Chronicles 23 • Psalm 29 – 30, Psalm 108

The coming of the Lord

What happens when Jesus returns? That's the question the Thessalonian Christians seem to have been asking.

These believers came from a culture in which the idea of a bodily resurrection was very strange. So they were confused. What happens to those who die before Jesus comes back?

Read 1 Thessalonians 4:13-18

> ❓ *What is the core belief which gives us confidence that we will rise from the dead (v 14)?*

Perhaps Paul's confidence in our future resurrection is why he calls those who have died "those who have fallen asleep". Death isn't permanent. When Jesus returns, all those who trusted in him in their lifetimes will be brought with him.

Some read this phrase as indicating "soul sleep"—the idea that when you die, you enter an unconscious state that lasts until Jesus' return. But it's clear from elsewhere that when we die, we are immediately in the presence of Christ—see Luke 16:22-23 and Philippians 1:21-23. It makes more sense to read "fallen asleep" as simply a metaphor for dying.

First in line

> ❓ *What will Jesus' return be like (1 Thessalonians 4:16)?*

> ❓ *What will happen to those who have already died (v 16) and those who are still alive (v 17)?*

This isn't floating around as an ethereal being in heaven for eternity; it's a real, physical, bodily resurrection. Most importantly, it involves being with the Lord for ever (v 17).

Encourage one another

> ❓ *What impact does Paul hope that these truths will have on the believers (v 13, 18)?*

> ❓ *What impact do they have on you today?*

Paul is not saying that Christians don't grieve. There is nothing wrong with grief! But we do grieve differently to those who have no hope. We can find comfort and strength in knowing that we will one day be with the Lord, reunited with our loved ones who fell asleep trusting that same Lord.

⌄ Apply

These encouragements aren't just for when we are grieving. They can encourage us at any time of anxiety or distress. Jesus said to his disciples, "Do not let your hearts be troubled" (John 14:1)—why? Because he was going to prepare a place for them. He told them, "I will come back and take you to be with me that you also may be where I am" (v 3).

Take some time to reflect on this. Pray for those you know who are bereaved or anxious in any way. Consider if there is something you could do to encourage or strengthen them.

Children of light

How do you prepare for Christ's return? That's what the Thessalonians want to know. That, and when he's coming.

Read 1 Thessalonians 5:1-3

❷ *What are the two metaphors Paul uses to describe the day of Jesus' return?*

❷ *What feelings do they conjure up as you read them?*

Jesus' return is as inevitable as a pregnant woman's labour pains, yet unpredictable. Even Jesus said he didn't know (Matthew 24:36)! The second coming is going to be sudden and surprising, especially for unbelievers. Very few people outside the church today have any kind of anticipation of a reckoning with God at the end. But it will happen.

⌃ Pray

Take a moment to pray for those you know who do not believe in Christ. Cry out to God for their salvation. Ask him also to make you more ready for Jesus' return as you study this passage.

You're not in darkness

The second coming will be a day that is hard for some. Wrongs will be righted and what is temporary will be destroyed. But along with judgment comes salvation. Sin and death will be no more, and those who have trusted in Jesus will begin to dwell with him eternally.

Read 1 Thessalonians 5:4-11

❷ *What encouragement does Paul offer in verses 4-5?*

❷ *What do you think he means by this?*

When Paul uses the word "darkness" here, he means moral darkness. Christians are not in the deadness of sin but have been saved by Christ.

❷ *And therefore what should we do (v 6-8, 11)?*

In verse 6, Paul doesn't mean literally awake. He means we need to live our lives in anticipation of the return of Christ—letting the hope of the second coming direct and govern everything else.

And when he says "sober," this isn't an indication that the Thessalonians had a drinking problem. It's part of Paul's metaphor. Bad things can happen at night—it's a picture of what spiritual darkness looks like. We are to live in line with the light; we are to live for Jesus, not for the world.

⌄ Apply

❷ *How do you think the second coming should affect what we value?*

❷ *How do you think the second coming should affect us when we encounter injustice and pain?*

❷ *How does verse 8 help us understand what it means to be "sober"—and what would it look like to put this into practice?*

Bible in a year: 1 Chronicles 26 – 27 • Psalm 131, Psalm 143

Living in peace

We all want to live at peace with others—but sometimes it's easier said than done.

Today's passage explores what positive, peaceful, Christian relationships look like.

Read 1 Thessalonians 5:12-15

❓ *What types of people does Paul mention in these verses?*

❓ *Can you think of people you know who fit these categories?*

The highest regard

Verses 12-13 don't use the words "pastor" or "elder", but those are the people we should understand Paul to be talking about. He means those who labour for, lead and teach their congregations. "Admonish" is translating a Greek word that can mean "warn" or "caution" but literally means "put in mind"—so it speaks of the pastor or elder's work in reminding others of what they know and what impact it should have in their lives.

❓ *Think about your church leaders. Can you think of some specific ways in which they are putting verse 12 into practice?*

❓ *How can you, in return, put verse 13 into practice?*

🔼 Pray

Take a moment to pray for your church leaders. Ask God to grow them in godliness, so that they can be effective in leading and teaching. Ask for God's help for your whole congregation to encourage your leaders.

Warn and encourage

Paul addresses his readers as "brothers and sisters"—signalling that a church should be a family. They should be unified and at peace (v 13).

❓ *Living at peace with others is sometimes challenging. How does Paul help us with that in verses 14-15?*

❓ *Which of these instructions do you think you find easiest, and which hardest, to obey?*

We are not to leave the job of encouraging and warning other Christians to church leaders. We are all to help each other—not throwing our weight around, but seeking to support others to live for Christ. We are all to be concerned about one another's spiritual wellbeing.

Three more words

Paul finishes verse 15 by looking outside the church. We are not just to do good to other Christians. Our standard posture towards the world should be to bless and do good.

🔼 Pray

Consider the instructions in these verses one by one. Ask God to show you how you, and your church more widely, could grow in putting these things into practice. Praise God for the ways in which he is already at work in your congregation.

Bible in a year: 1 Chronicles 28 • Revelation 11 • Psalm 111, Psalm 127

Last reminders

We all need nudges to do the things that we know we need to do. The ending of 1 Thessalonians is packed full of such nudges.

Read 1 Thessalonians 5:16-28

Follow God's will

People often ask what the Lord's will is for their life. Who should they marry? Where should they live? But in verses 16-18 we see very clearly one aspect of God's will for us. We are to rejoice, present requests to God, and give thanks continually.

⌃ Pray

Take some time to put that into practice now. Consider, too, what might help you to develop habits of rejoicing and giving thanks continually.

Be discerning

In verses 19-22 Paul is referring to when people claim that they have a specific word from God. These claims aren't always true! So the Thessalonians should "test" what they hear carefully in the light of Scripture. At the same time, they should not automatically reject prophetic words, but be prepared to listen to what is good.

Commentators disagree on whether this still happens in our day, but these verses definitely apply to us. "Do not quench the Spirit": that means don't resist the Spirit's daily work of building God's church, equipping us to live in line with God's will, and reminding us of our salvation. Don't ignore the Spirit's prompting or disobey God.

❓ *Can you think of a time when you have been tempted to "quench the Spirit" in that sense?*

⌃ Pray

The verses we've read so far have invited us to reflect on our prayer life and our faith. But Paul adds a crucial reminder that it is not all up to us.

Read through verses 23-24 slowly—maybe do so a few times. Then pray this prayer for yourself. Add your own prayers of rejoicing and gratitude as you reflect on what you've read.

Parting requests

❓ *What are Paul's last few requests to the Thessalonians?*

❓ *What about you? How do you think readers today can put these words into practice?*

In Paul's time, a "holy kiss" was an expression of love and fellowship. If we come from a culture where a kiss is not a normal greeting, we don't need to start kissing each other in order to obey Paul's teaching here! The important thing is simply to convey affection in the way we greet one another. After all, the gospel makes us into one family.

❓ *Think back over the whole letter. Who could you encourage with a thought from 1 Thessalonians this week?*

God save the King

They may not realise they're doing it, but when Britons sing, "God save the King", they sing a prayer not only for the monarch but also for the nation.

The idea is that the blessing of a people and its ruler are inseparable. So too here.

Read Psalm 20

The king is heading into battle. Here the people cry out to the Lord, asking for victory for the king (v 1-5, 9). In verses 6-9 we are probably hearing the voice of the king responding, declaring his own trust—and as their representative and leader, declaring the nation's trust—in the Lord.

The hopes of the people are clearly bound up with the victory of the king over his enemies (v 5, 9). If their prayers are heard and the king is victorious over his foes, the people will be assured that God is indeed on their side.

Like all the psalms of David that speak of the "king", or the "anointed" one (see v 6), this psalm points us ultimately to Jesus, God's great anointed King.

David had undoubtedly offered many sacrifices and burnt offerings to the Lord (v 3), and the people trust that the Lord will look favourably on those and so support him in battle. As we see Jesus in the psalm, we remember that he has offered the great sacrifice at the cross.

❓ *Looking back at the cross, how do we know that God has accepted Jesus' sacrifice? How did the Lord give victory to King Jesus?*

❓ *What assurance does his victory give us for today and for the future?*

❓ *What does it mean that the enemies of God will "fall" and his people will "rise up and stand firm" (v 8)? When will that ultimately happen?*

⌄ Apply

❓ *When and where have you been putting your trust in "chariots" and "horses"— that is, in worldly sources of strength and protection?*

❓ *What truths from Psalm 20 have you forgotten or failed to believe, leading to your misplaced trust?*

❓ *What will it look like for you to turn to and trust in Jesus instead of those "chariots" and "horses" that you've just identified?*

⌃ Pray

Praise the Lord for the victory he has given to Jesus, his King.

Confess ways in which you have put your trust and confidence in people and things, but not in the Lord.

Ask the Lord to help you to trust in him wholeheartedly; ask for help to do that particularly in areas where you see you have not been doing so.

FAITHFULLY PRESENT

Embracing the limits of
where and when God has you

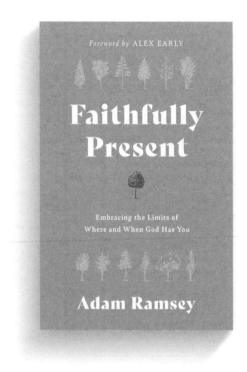

Most of us feel that life is rushing past. Often we're
so busy thinking about the next thing that we risk
missing the people and places God has put in front
of us. This book shows us how to live each day fully
and faithfully present with God and with others.

thegoodbook.co.uk/faithfully-present
thegoodbook.com/faithfully-present

1 & 2 THESSALONIANS FOR YOU

Expository guide to

Paul's letters to the Thessalonian church

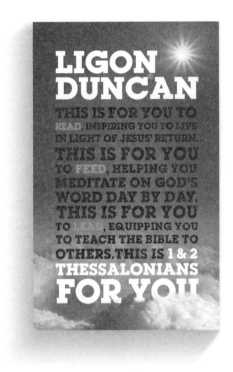

Pastor and professor Ligon Duncan unpacks these
two letters verse by verse, teaching us about living
in the light of Christ's future return. This accessible
commentary is useful for personal devotion and
leading group Bible studies or sermon preparation.

thegoodbook.co.uk/thess-for-you
thegoodbook.com/thess-for-you

Introduce a friend to

explore

If you're enjoying using *Explore*, why not introduce a friend? Time with God is our introduction to daily Bible reading and is a great way to get started with a regular time with God. It includes 28 daily readings along with articles, advice and practical tips on how to apply what the passage teaches.

Why not order a copy for someone you would like to encourage?

Coming up next...

- Daniel
  with Tim Thornborough and Rachel Jones

- 2 Thessalonians
  with Ligon Duncan and Katy Morgan

- Romans
  with Timothy Keller

- Jeremiah
  with Dave Griffith-Jones

Don't miss your copy. Contact your local Christian bookshop or church agent, or visit:

UK & Europe: thegoodbook.co.uk
info@thegoodbook.co.uk
Tel: 0333 123 0880

North America: thegoodbook.com
info@thegoodbook.com
Tel: 866 244 2165

Australia & New Zealand:
thegoodbook.com.au
info@thegoodbook.com.au
Tel: (02) 9564 3555

South Africa: www.christianbooks.co.za
orders@christianbooks.co.za
Tel: 021 674 6931/2